With his extensive knowledge of history, wonderfully insightful stories, and characteristic wit, Dennis teaches us that though not everyone can be a legend, we all have the opportunity and responsibility to leave a godly legacy.

Dr. Charles Stanley, *Senior Pastor*
First Baptist Church of Atlanta, Atlanta, GA

Dennis has a funny way of getting us thinking about serious things. His qualifications as an arborist may be uncertain, but I've been personally blessed and encouraged by the seeds he has planted in my own life and the lives of those around me. His exhortation to consider our daily words, actions, and priorities in light of their eternal impact on others is not some shady idea—it's Biblical. I appreciate that Dennis is not an academic hypothesizing about all of this. He speaks from personal experience as a planter mentored by planters. I pray that as you read these chapters you will be strengthened in your faith and encouraged to sow seeds in the lives of others that will bring glory to God in this generation, generations to come, and for eternity.

Bruce Smith, *President*
Wycliffe Associates, Orlando, FL

Dennis has been planting shade trees all over the world for decades. Recently Dennis encouraged our members to plant a few shade trees here, and a few months later those "trees" produced $135 million in fruit for the kingdom of God! This book is a "must-read" for every pastor and layman interested in r̲ ̲ ̲ ̲ ̲ ̲rnal difference with his life.

First

Dennis Swanberg's deep insight into the importance of investing in eternity comes to life in his new book. If you want to leave a spiritual legacy for others, read *Planting Shade Trees*.

Dr. David Jeremiah, *Senior Pastor*
Shadow Mountain Community Church, El Cajon, CA

Dennis Swanberg's *Planting Shade Trees* message helped motivate our church (that had never committed over $1.5 million) to commit $12.5 million. It was the week following the stock market crash and the worst economy since the Great Depression. I have seen God use *Planting Shade Trees* to move His people from fear to faith, leaving a lasting legacy.

Dr. Grant Ethridge, *Senior Pastor*
Liberty Baptist Church, Hampton, VA

The best life lessons I have learned are those that are true, simple and come from God's Word. Dennis Swanberg's book *Planting Shade Trees* can be characterized in this way. Dennis makes deep, theological concepts understandable while adding his characteristic humor. This book teaches truths that we can live by!

Dr. John Ed Mathison, *Senior Pastor (Ret.)*
Frazer Memorial United Methodist Church, Montgomery, AL

We have had the privilege of having Dennis speak at our signature major donor events dozens and dozens of times. We always request the "shade tree" talk, as we have found this message really forms thinking of transformational giving in the hearts of the donors who attend our events.

Bob Westfall, President, *Westfall Group*

PLANTING SHADE TREES

Published by Swanberg, Inc.
Monroe, Louisiana 71201

Scripture references marked NLT are from the Holy Bible. New Living Translation. Copyright © 1996 Tyndale Charitable Trust. Used by permission of Tyndale House Publishers.

Scripture references marked NASB are from the Holy Bible. The New American Standard Bible®. Copyright © 1960, 1962, 1963, 1968, 1971, 1972, 1973, 1975, 1977, 1995 by The Lockman Foundation. Used by permission.

Cover Design by Kim Russell / Wahoo Designs
Page Layout by Bart Dawson

Printed in the United States of America

2 3 4 5—CHG—18 17 16 15

PLANTING SHADE TREES

DR. DENNIS SWANBERG

I want to dedicate this book
to my PARTNER IN LIFE,
LAUREE WILKES SWANBERG, who has
"PLANTED SHADE TREES" with me
since MAY 19, 1979!

TABLE OF CONTENTS

SPECIAL THANKS TO SHADE-TREE PLANTERS

So many family members and friends have planted shade trees for me that I would run out of space trying to mention them all. But, you know who you are. And, I'm grateful for you!

Four special families have believed in our Ministry of Encouragement and in the need for this book. These families have helped make this project possible through their support and prayers. I want to offer special thanks to these world-class shade-tree planters: Paul and Stacy Spence, Andy and Joan (with the Lord in heaven now) Horner, Tim and Peggy Horner, and Sid and Charline Wilhite.

There's one more group I must thank: the churches that allowed me to be their pastor. These churches and their key shade-tree planters influenced me to be all that I am today as a planter in the Kingdom work.

First Baptist Church, Rogers, Texas, took a young preacher boy and his new bride and allowed us to grow and learn while planting seeds in people's lives in central Texas. But my next-door neighbor—deacon and U.S. postmaster of Rogers—Wray Durnal was my shade-tree planter. He loved me, encouraged me, guided me, and constantly told me that God was going to use me in a grand way in His Kingdom. He was a layman who left a legacy on my life—a saint under the radar—and who is now grinning from the balcony of heaven!

First Baptist Church, Saginaw, Texas, gave me the opportunity to grow and spread my wings. While serving there,

God gave me Wade Freeman, a "Big Brother"—a man who believed in me and once told me, "As long as you don't do anything immoral or steal from the cookie jar, I'm with you 100%; I'll do whatever you ask me to do!" Wade and his wife LouAnn and their sons Russ and Brad and their families have always been in my "Shade Tree Corner." Wade is still encouraging me from the balcony of heaven. Oh how he planted shade trees for me!

Second Baptist Church, Hot Springs, Arkansas, matured me—enabled me to discover my "Encouraging Gifts" while leading the church at the same time. Three men were always there for me, building me up, keeping me accountable, being "Forever Friends": Jim Smith, Joe Wilson, and Thomas Glover. They—as well as their wives—were there for me, and still are. Oh how I enjoy their shade!

First Baptist Church, West Monroe, Louisiana, was my "Swan's Song" of shade-tree planting. I knew deep down that my tenure might not be as long as I would like it to be—but the good news is that I was able to "Plant for the Future"! My shade-tree planter was Perry Daniels. Perry owned the local appliance store—and was selling furniture and appliances into his '80s! But his true calling was planting shade trees for First Baptist in purchasing properties for the church's future expansion. When I first arrived, he asked me, "Preacher, how do you feel about buying property around the church?" I said, "I think we need all of it—or as much as we can get for the future of the church if the Lord tarries." Mr. Daniels said, "I'm glad you feel that way; I do too!" So, I said, "Perry, go buy it!" Perry Daniels had developed untold relationships with home and property owners for decades, and in my four years at FBC, we purchased 24 pieces of property—even bought a country club to serve as an activities center. This octogenarian was not on dead center! As a result of his forward shade-tree planting, we now have the parking space and building space that has accommodated 3,000 instead of 1,200. I love and miss Perry Daniel. He's probably on the "building committee" of heaven's mansions!

And please permit me to mention one last shade-tree planter who has prayed for me faithfully in the early hours of the morning before he would carry out his U.S. postal carrier duties in Hot Springs, Arkansas, since 1987. His name is Mike Karber. Not only does he pray for me, but he sends "prayer notes" to me just when I need them. Each one is marked with "4:00 a.m." and includes words that have kept me going in the "worst and best of times"—there is a friend who sticketh closer than a brother. Thank you, brother Mike, for all your prayers. Please keep praying!

I know, there are hundreds of other shade-tree planters in my life! I thank God for all of them, and I thank God now for YOU because I know that hopefully YOU will be planting even more shade trees as a result of reading this book. Shade trees that you may never sit under . . . but others will.

Thanks to all my shade-tree planter friends!

—Dennis

SENSITIVITY

SURRENDER

SILVER

SIGHT

SIGNATURE

INTRODUCTION

MY GREAT-GRANDFATHER
PLANTED SHADE TREES FOR ME

My family tree has its roots in Sweden. Both sides of my family—the Swanbergs and the Johnsons—are Swedish. My great-grandpa Aron Johnson came to the United States in the 1880s. He and my great-grandmother Carolina Johnson eventually settled in Texas. They settled down in a little community called Manda, which is east of Austin. Manda happens to be just three miles from another hamlet called New Sweden. So, my great-grandparents traveled half way around the world and still managed to find neighbors who spoke their language. The home they constructed on a 120-acre farm still remains.

After my great-grandfather built the homeplace, he planted some shade trees and some fruit trees. But, when my grandfather, Carl Johnson, was only five years old, my great-grandfather passed away.

Aron Johnson planted shade trees that he never sat under. . . . but his wife did, and his boy (my grandfather) did, and my mother did, too. And, I've had the pleasure of sitting beneath those trees with my two sons. You get the picture: the family has enjoyed those shade trees for over 100 years.

Oh, the power of trees! But Aron Johnson didn't just plant the kind of trees that drop leaves in the fall. He also planted shade trees of faith, family, and a future of hope.

I am the recipient of those who have gone before me. And I've often said to myself, "How can I ever repay them?" I realize I can't return to 19th-century Texas and say, "Thank you," to my forebears. But what I can do is this: I can carry on the tradition of planting shade trees. And that's exactly what I intend to do as long as the Lord gives me the strength to plant them.

In the first half of this text, I explore several ideas about planting shade trees because I believe that you are a shade-tree planter, too. Then, in the final nine chapters, I'll focus on Jeremiah 32, which contains an amazing story about a godly man. I've been preaching about Jeremiah's adventure in shade-tree planting for over 30 years, and the message is just as meaningful today as it was when I was a wet-behind-the-ears seminary student.

So this is what I want you to do: go get yourself a cup of coffee—latte if you prefer—or a soft drink. Then, sit back and read about all kinds of shade trees, and about the truths that "shadow" them.

And, may God inspire you to be just like Him: an eternal Shade-Tree Planter!

5 ESSENTIAL ELEMENTS OF A SHADE-TREE PLANTER

SENSITIVITY
You must be sensitive to God's voice;

SURRENDER
You must surrender to God's calling;

SILVER
You must be willing to invest your time,
your talents, and your money;

SIGHT
You must have a vision of the future,
a mental image of God's plan for your unique gift
or your particular contribution;

SIGNATURE
When the time for action comes, you must be
willing to sign your name and seal your pledge.

CHAPTER 1

LESSONS FROM A WALK IN THE WOODS

I like to drive over the Golden Gate Bridge from San Francisco to Marin County, the ritzy county just north of the City by the Bay. While I'm driving across the bridge, I have to make myself pay attention to my lane because I'm always tempted to look right, over the orange rail, at Alcatraz. You know me: a little A.D.D.

When I get to the north end of the bridge I immediately start looking for the turnoff to the Muir Woods. The Muir Woods are a copse of coastal redwood trees down some steep switchbacks descending into the hills that wind up at the Pacific Ocean. At the very bottom of a valley, at the end of that road, you can drive into an enchanted forest. There you can find one of the largest stands of thousand-year-old trees in the world. These are not the giant sequoias you can find at Yosemite Park—these are their country cousins.

These giant coastal redwood trees sprouted halfway back to the time of Jesus. When these trees were saplings, King

Arthur and Sir Lancelot hadn't yet done their thing at the round table. These trees were 500 years old when Columbus hit the beach in the West Indies. They are older than Methuselah, the oldest man in history. No doubt about it: these redwoods are *old*.

When you walk into the Muir Woods, a strange and mysterious silence surrounds you. A comforting peace blankets you. I cannot explain it. Maybe this is what the Garden of Eden was like before the apple.

The trees stand like silent sentinels filtering the sun through green leaves. Wisps of fog gather above you. Quiet streams flow beside you. People whisper as if they were in church.

As I walk through the woods, I like to stop and read the signs. You know the signs I'm talking about: those informative markers that give directions and describe the scenery. Not surprisingly, I always seem to learn something new. For example, I thought that trees so tall would have roots going halfway to China. Actually, this is not the case. The roots from one tree reach out and "shake hands" with roots from another tree. These millennial trees stand up because they hold one another up. That's why you don't find them growing by themselves like Lone Ranger trees. There are no Maverick coastal redwood trees. They stand for so long because they stand together and hold one another up.

It's like God to put a truth so clearly in front of our noses that none of us could deny it. God wants us to be like giant redwoods, standing tall because we support each other.

Many of us, especially those of us who are macho men, want to leave the impression that we go it alone. We are rough, tough, and sure enough. We are a bag of chips and all of that. We're John Wayne, Clint Eastwood, and Batman with no Robin. We are the Lone Ranger without Tonto and Sherlock without Dr. Watson. We don't need *anybody*. When the going gets tough we're the tough hombres who get going. We tell ourselves and everybody else, "If you can't stand the heat get out of the kitchen." Yet deep down, in the middle of the night, we know we need others.

> God wants us to be like giant redwoods, standing tall because we support each other.

The next time you're tempted to go it alone, remember those coastal redwoods. And if you're ever in the neighborhood, take a walk in the Muir Woods. The trees testify. They tell us that to last we have to intertwine our roots and hold one another up.

TOGETHER, WE'RE STRONGER . . . AND BETTER

The Bible does indeed say, "Let each man bear his own burden" (Gal. 6:5). Yet it also says, "Bear one another's burdens" (Gal. 6:2). If I am bearing your burden and you are bearing mine, we are holding one another up.

The Bible also says, "Cast your burden on the Lord" (1 Pet. 5:7). Adding this verse to the previous two verses from Galatians, we now have an interesting trio. If I carry my own burden, I don't have to give it to you. If you do the same, you don't have to give your burden to me. Yet at the same time we are to bear one another's burdens. We can do so by casting *all* burdens, both yours *and* mine, on the Lord.

There are times when the Jesus in me needs the Jesus in you. The Christ in me grows weak by my own lack of trust, and I need the Christ in you—I need to witness your robust trust. We need one another.

If you take any one piece of metal off of an aircraft carrier and throw it into the ocean, the scrapped piece of metal will sink. But, when a shipbuilder welds millions of pieces of metal together, the result is a floating city with 4,000 people onboard.

Consider the chemical formula for common salt: NaCl (sodium chloride). If you take either sodium or chloride by itself, what you get is an element that's unstable, poisonous, and unsafe. But when you put sodium and chloride together, you've got salt, a compound without which you and I cannot live, and without which, our foods taste bland. The helpfulness of sodium and chloride rests in their being together.

Our need for one another comes out in cold statistics. Do you know which folks are the most at risk of early death? Divorced folks face a 23% great likelihood of early death. And, men over 45 who live alone have higher mortality rates than their married counterparts. It seems that God has made us to be interdependent, to need another so much that we risk a shorter stay on earth if we don't have someone to lean on. We need to intertwine our roots with someone else, or some living thing, in order to survive.

There are times when the Jesus in me needs the Jesus in you.

FACING THE FIRE

There was another thing "The Swan" learned walking through the Muir Woods. I learned that trees actually *need* a forest fire from time to time.

Years ago the rangers tried to prevent forest fires at all costs. Then, they learned a lesson. Without fires, the floor of the forest builds up piles of rotting leaves, fungus, and other harmful stuff. So, an occasional forest fire is actually a good thing because it cleanses the floor of the forest and destroys the threatening debris. Those thousand-year-old coastal red-woods need a fire now and then to keep the rot from hurting them.

None of us like fires in life, but we all have them. Old Job said, "Man is born to trouble as surely as the sparks fly upward" (Job 5:7). Jesus put it even more clearly: "In this world you will have tribulation" (John 16:33). The question is not *whether* you will be forced to endure hardship, but *when*.

Tough times, by the way, can actually have very positive results. You cannot polish a gemstone without friction. You can't make an omelet without breaking a few eggs. And, as a wise old preacher once said, "You can't climb a smooth mountain." It is the crags and the gorges, the cracks and crevices, that enable you to get a foothold on the mountain.

After a lifetime of serving Jesus, Peter wrote, "Do not be surprised at the painful trial" (1 Pet. 4:2). My grandfather Swanberg had great a big fire pit in an old 55-gallon drum. When the family would stand outside around the fire, every now and then the flames would begin to whistle. We kids did not have a clue what was happening. Grandpa would tell us how some air was trapped in the log. The heat from the fire would release the music inside. He said, "Kids, it takes the fire to bring out the music."

What's true for fire pits is also true in life. Fires can, and often do, bring out the music. And, they can clean out the undergrowth in our lives. When trials and troubles come our way, we become focused in a hurry. We make the main thing the main thing. Lesser things get burned out of us, and that is good.

Fires do another strange thing in the forest: they give the trees an opportunity for new life. Those Monterrey Pines have closed cones that are sealed by sap. The seeds build up in the pine cone for years. When a forest fire provides heat, the sap melts, the cones open, and they drop their seeds the day after the fire. Without the fire, the seeds might never drop. It is the fire that brings regeneration; it is the heat that provides new life. Without the fire there would be no new trees. God has built it into nature and into life: those fiery trials can produce more life.

When Michelangelo painted his masterpiece on the ceiling of the Sistine Chapel, he did so while in great pain. Do you remember that old movie *The Agony and the Ecstasy*, the one where Charlton Heston played Michelangelo? Old Charlton spent the better part of that movie lying on his back, high up on a rickety scaffold, with paintbrush in hand, working despite great anguish. And don't forget that those were the days before extra-strength Tylenol!

Meanwhile, as Heston suffered, Rex Harrison, as the Pope, demanded the master paint faster, and faster, and faster. A lesser man might have punted, but not Heston-as-Michelangelo. Old Charlton never backed down, he never backed up, and he never called in sick. The master just kept painting. And the result was transcendent beauty that came out of his pain. His stress resulted in great art.

Another art form that requires stress is music. Consider the way a grand piano makes music. I talked to my friend of over 40 years, Dr. Benjamin Harlan, past dean of Southwestern Baptist Theological Seminary and professor of New Orleans Seminary. He's also a great pianist and composer of sacred music. He said a grand piano has 230 strings. Those strings produce a total tensile stress of 30 tons. That is, the metal harp that holds the pins that stretch the strings is quietly holding back the equivalent of 30 tons of weight underneath the lid of the piano.

If that harp inside the piano were suddenly to crack, it would blow through the ceiling like an 18 wheeler. Yet, here is the strange truth: it takes the stress to make the music. If there were no stress on the strings, we would only hear a dull thud when the felt-covered hammer hit the strings. Yep, it takes the stress to make the music, both on pianos and in life. That must have been what Paul meant when he wrote, "This light, momentary tribulation is working out an eternal weight of glory beyond all comparison" (2 Cor. 4:17).

Dr. Harlan also reminded me how close a bright major key chord is to a sad minor key chord. It is only one-half step. If you plan C-E-G you have a sunny, crisp, major key chord. All you have to do is slide that E into an E-flat and suddenly you have a melancholy minor key sound. Life is often like that. You are only one-half step away from a different day. Yet God uses those changes to make you who you are.

When I think of great music, I'm often reminded of Tom Chisholm. Tom never achieved what the world might call success. He tried his hand at editing, but that job didn't last. He attempted part-time insurance sales and that didn't work out either. Even a try at pastoring did not last for long. Yet this rather frail looking man sat down on a day and penned the words that will outlive him for centuries. A million people sing it in multiple languages every Sunday. It is always on the list of favorite hymns. You probably sing it often. You see, Tom Chisholm wrote *Great Is Thy Faithfulness*.

My favorite verse in Tom's hymn tells us of God's faithfulness in every season and every fire:

Summer and winter, and springtime and harvest,
Sun, moon and stars in their courses above,
Join with all nature in manifold witness
To Thy great faithfulness, mercy and love.

The next time you have a chance to walk in the woods, listen closely. When you're alone with nature, you can almost hear the trees sing those words. The glories of nature remind us that God, the Creator, has a beautiful plan for each of us, even when we are being tested by fire.

TWO IMPORTANT TRUTHS

My walk in the Muir Woods taught me two very important truths. First, I was reminded that, in this world, we need to hold one another up. Second, I learned that some fires can be healthy because they have a cleansing and focusing effect on our lives.

You can plant shade trees that others can sit under if you hold one another up and if you recognize that the fires of life only furnish focus.

CHAPTER 2

SHADE TREES AND ME

Not long ago, I visited Grandpa Swanberg's farm and gazed upon trees he planted nearly a hundred years ago. Those trees have seen two world wars, Pearl Harbor, the turbulent 1960s, the tragedy of 9/11, and every president since Teddy Roosevelt. A funny thing struck me while I was sitting on my granddad's old bench watching the wind sweep the upper branches of those shade trees: Grandpa's trees survived it all, thrived in it all, and will probably even outlast me.

Here I am, made in God's image, and a doggone tree will outlive me. It's ironic, to say the least, and I'm not the only guy who ever thought about it. Job had the same idea when he was arguing with God about all his troubles.

Job asked God why He would heap so much adversity upon someone as weak as himself. Job was having a self-catered pity party. Job reminded God that he was only a leaf, some stubble, a shadow, and fading flower (Job 13:25–14:2).

Then Job had the same thought that I had sitting under Grandpa's trees:

For there is hope for a tree,
If it is cut down, that it will sprout again,
And that its tender roots not cease.
Though its root may grow old in the earth,
And its stump may die in the ground,
Yet at the scent of water it will bud
And bring forth branches like a plant
But man dies and is laid away;
Indeed he breathes his last
And where is he?
(Job 14:7-10)

By the way, it may not be your best day when you envy a tree.

So, it's pretty clear that Job was having a bad time of it when he spoke those words to God. Job made note of the fact that every person on this planet comes in with an "expires-on" date. Job was well aware of a great truth that each of us tends to avoid: we will all leave here.

We leave one-at-a-time and sometimes through crevices so narrow that we are scarred in the leaving. We enter life alone, and we leave it alone, and we all do leave. As Tony Campolo says, "One day they will put you in a box, put the box in a box, put you in the ground, and go back to the church, eat fried chicken and potato salad and talk about you." Tony certainly knows how to make a point. Like George Strait's song, "I never saw a hearse with a U-Haul on its rack."

Ray Stedman once showed up to preach, but his luggage got lost en route. He didn't have a suit back in the dark ages when preachers all wore suits. The local preacher told Ray not to worry; a suit would be delivered. Sure enough, a man showed up with a new suit in time for church. Ray put on the suit, reached for his billfold to put into the back pocket and then made a startling discovery: the suit had no pockets. Not on the sides or on the back. Ray put down his wallet, ran to church, and got ready to preach. After the service he asked the preacher what kind of suit it was with no pockets. The preacher reluctantly told Ray, "Well, I hate to tell you this, but it came from the funeral home."

When we die, we won't take anything with us. Yet, we can all leave something behind.

When we die, we won't take anything with us. Yet, we can all leave something behind.

As I sat on my grandfather's bench, I was reminded that even though he is gone, he left plenty behind, including those trees he planted on the barren Texas landscape a hundred years ago. What are some things you can leave behind? One thing you can leave behind is this: *You can leave behind evidence of a life of faithfulness.* Steven Green's ballad peels out this truth:

> *Oh may all who come behind us find us faithful*
> *May the fire of our devotion light their way*
> *May the footprints that we leave*
> *Lead them to believe*
> *And the lives we live inspire them to obey*
> *Oh may all who come behind us find us faithful*

Job envied a tree, but no one today remembers that tree; they remember the legacy of Job. All over the planet people read his book in hundreds of languages but no one visits Job's tree. When I look at Grandpa's trees, I'm reminded that he left behind a legacy more important than a whole forest. Grandpa left behind a legacy of faithfulness. The papers, the pictures, the family heirlooms, the odds and ends of a lifetime now remind four generations that his life was a shining example of faithfulness.

THE TREASURES WE LEAVE BEHIND

Someday, my sons will go through my stuff. They will sort, discuss, divide it up, and keep some of it. Riffling through desks, files, old papers, clippings, and all the rest, I want them to find one particular treasure: I want them to find evidence that I was faithful. What will happen when folks go through your stuff? Will they find that you left something longer lasting than a tree?

Karl Kisner was sorting through his granddad's attic shortly after his grandfather had passed. Under an old birdcage he found a soot-covered box. He opened it and found some baseball cards from a hundred years ago. They were smaller than today's cards, held together by twine and still in the box. He looked at a few. There was one for Ty Cobb, another for Cy Young, and still another for Honus Wagner.

Kinser put the cards aside and continued looking for something valuable in the attic. Only later did he discover that he and his cousins had found one of the biggest finds in sport's trading card history, worth millions. It was a mint-condition set of some of the rarest cards in baseball trading card history.

There is something more important that you can leave in your attic than any trading card collection. It is a legacy of faithfulness to Jesus and to His mission.

You can leave behind something that expands your own influence.

Job felt flimsy, temporary, and marginal and like a leaf blowing in the wind. Yet Job left behind a book of 42 chapters that belongs to the ages. You, like Job, can leave behind a permanent legacy, so never underestimate the durability of the treasures you can leave behind.

For years I have read a little book by Oswald Chambers. Millions of people read this book every morning. It's printed in many languages. You probably know this book by name, and you may even own a copy. It's called *My Utmost for His Highest*. The book, which provides a devotional reading for every day of the year, is one of the most influential Christian texts ever written.

Oswald was a Scot born in Aberdeen in 1874. Few people knew him during his lifetime. He was an artist, a teacher at a small Bible college, and a travelling preacher. When World War I broke out, Chambers volunteered to go to Cairo as a chaplain for the troops affiliated with the YMCA. He brought his bride along, and in a little hut, nothing more than a lean-to, he taught a handful of troops who listened to his striking devotional teachings before they went to the trenches to die.

In 1917, Chambers died after an emergency appendectomy. He was just 41 years old. The pyramids looked down on the little camp where he perished. There lay a nobody, just another anonymous corpse, the earthly remains of a totally unimportant man. Oswald Chambers, like so many men before him, lived, and died, and left no evidence of his passing. He was like Job's leaf in the wind. Or so it seemed.

Thankfully, the story didn't end there.

You see, Chamber's bride Gertrude could take dictation at a phenomenal 150 words per minute. In that desert hut by the pyramids, she wrote down everything her young groom told the little gathering of soldiers. After Oswald died, she returned to Oxford and ran a boarding house. Every morning, after the tenants left, she went into the basement and, on an old manual typewriter, transcribed her shorthand notes. She shaped those notes into the daily readings that the world now knows as *My Utmost for His Highest*. Even though it appeared, at the time of his death, that Oswald had vanished into eternity, he left behind a shade tree that blesses millions every day.

CHAPTER 3

EVERYBODY NEEDS SOMEBODY

No man is an island,
Entire of itself.
Each is a piece of the continent,
A part of the main.

J ohn Donne wrote those unforgettable words. You are not an island. And you will not live your life alone. The life you choose to live, and the example you set, will make a lasting impression on the people around you.

One person who planted a shade tree for me was Dr. Marshall Edwards, the man called "Rabbi." Rabbi was the team chaplain of our state-championship football team at John H. Reagan High School, Austin, Texas. He is the man who pointed me to Jesus Christ. Better yet, he was one who "planted a seed" of salvation for me as I entered my junior year of high school.

When Marshall Edwards attended high school in Covington, Georgia, he was blessed with a senior English teacher named Miss Mary Leila Ellington, an unassuming woman who spent her entire career in the public school system. Miss Mary was quiet but observant. And, she took notice of young Marshall Edwards. Miss Ellington had a holy hunch that Marshall had great promise.

When it was time for Marshall to go to college, his father wanted him to take an appointment to West Point. Marshall was even offered a scholarship to Harvard. But the Lord was leading Marshall to Baylor University to prepare himself for the gospel ministry.

When Marshall announced his plans to attend Baylor, his father replied, "If you are going to do a stupid thing like that, you can do it all by yourself!"

I can't imagine how my mentor must have felt at that young age. He was all alone. Just him and the Lord.

I was so blessed to have such supportive parents. Marshall was not so blessed. But a single faithful soul plus God equals a majority. God is the great orchestrator of Shade-Tree Planters.

During these difficult days, Marshall was down but determined—and he was never alone. God touched Miss Mary's heart and led this never-married woman of modest means—Miss Ellington never made over $5,000 a year—to assist Marshall with his education.

When Marshall began his fall semester, he was surprised to learn that an "anonymous gift" would help him pay the costs of attending Baylor. Unknown to Marshall, it was Miss Mary Leila Ellington who had sent the check. And, at the beginning of each year, another check arrived, anonymously, just like clockwork. For four years, Miss Ellington supported Marshall Edwards, allowing him to fulfill an opportunity far beyond his means and expectations. Every time Marshall Edwards stood to preach Miss Ellington was standing there too. She was invisible but very much present.

As Paul Harvey would say, "Now for the rest of the story!"

In 1972, I was awarded a four-year football and baseball scholarship to Lamar University in Beaumont, Texas. I went down for football that fall, but after a week, I was more than a little homesick. Most of all, as a young believer in Christ Jesus, I just didn't feel that Beaumont, Texas was where I needed to be.

I made many phone calls to my parents and to "Rabbi." It was the biggest phone bill in the history of the Swanberg family. My father, Floyd Leon, talked about that bill for years! Ultimately it was up to me and the Lord, and the verse He gave me was Psalm 37:4: "Delight thyself in the Lord and He will give you the desires of your heart." So I decided to return home.

I told my coach, Vernon Glass—brother of All-Pro B.U. grad Bill Glass—and Coach Glass understood. He told me before I left, "Don't look back, because if you do, you might miss God's very best that is right there in front of you!"

I climbed into my '64 White Chevy Impala with red interior and turned that stirring wheel toward Austin, Texas, and *never* looked back. When I arrived home that Wednesday night, my mom and dad greeted me in the driveway and said "welcome home . . . we love you!" Then my dad, my hero, the man I never wanted to let down, said, "'Rabbi' is going to take you and me to Baylor on Friday. He says you still need to go to college."

I couldn't believe it! After missing my first "big chance" in Beaumont, I might still become the first Swanberg boy to ever attend college. And to make things even more unbelievable, I was being driven to school by a young Baptist preacher (the "Rabbi") who was chauffeuring a Methodist father and son to the largest Baptist University in the whole wide world.

By the end of the day on Friday I was enrolled at Baylor University in Waco, Texas. School began the following Tuesday. Oh, the difference a day makes. That day changed my life. "Rabbi"—a thirty-something preacher who took his day off for a young man who was not even a member of his church—*CHANGED DENNIS SWANBERG'S WORLD!*

Little did I know that Dr. Edwards was talking with the pastoral search committee of Columbus Avenue Baptist Church in Waco about becoming their pastor. At that time, I didn't know how Baptist churches "called" a pastor—or more simply stated: "stole" a pastor—from another church.

A few of months later, "Rabbi" Edwards became one of the youngest and, as things turned out one of the most effective, pastors in the history of Columbus Avenue.

On his first day as pastor in November 1972, I walked the aisle and became a Baptist. Who would have ever "thunk it"—ha! Next thing I knew, those Baptists "put me under till I bubbled" (they baptized me!). Marshall was the one who put me under. I had on a white robe—kind of a Culottes outfit—and there I went down into those baptismal waters in the name of the Father, the Son, and the Holy Ghost. Matter of fact, he held me under till I said "TITHE!" (Baptists don't tell you that until they get you *under* the water!).

Later, Dr. Edwards asked me to be the minister to youth at that church. God must have a sense of humor. A Methodist boy from Austin goes a hundred miles up the interstate to Waco, winds up under water in a Baptist church, and then gets asked to be a youth minister to a bunch of kids while going to the world's largest Baptist university. God has a strange way of making divine prearrangements. He arranged for a whale to swallow Jonah; He made sure that a donkey was tied up just when Jesus needed one, and He arranged a whole new life for me.

In that moment at Columbus Avenue when Marshall put me under the water, Miss Mary Leila Ellington was there, too. She wasn't there in person, but she was there in spirit.

You see, Miss Ellington's good works helped transform Marshall Edward's life, and then his good works helped transform mine.

Contained in that particular moment were other important milestones in my life: Southwestern Seminary, a ministry job at the church across from the seminary, my first pastorate, meeting the girl I would marry, my sons, my whole larger life in entertainment, television, media, and speaking. Had Miss Ellington not sent Marshall to Baylor, I would not have been there either. Miss Ellington was planting another shade tree, and she did not even know it. Mrs. Ellington planted a shade tree for me. I can't wait to thank her in heaven!

Marshall Edwards remains my Father in the Ministry. He has retired to Blowing Rock, North Carolina, but he also resides in me. There's not a day that goes by that I don't notice the shadows of his influence on my life as I seek to plant shade trees for others. And oftentimes, I am reminded that the legacy of love began with Miss Ellington when planting faith, hope, and love in Marshall's young life.

> God has a strange way of making divine prearrangements.

By the way, while Marshall was pastor in Austin, before he left for Waco, Miss Ellington finally surprised him by revealing that she was the donor of all those checks. She had planned never to tell him, but while going through some old boxes of business papers and old checks, she saw the first check she had sent Baylor on Marshall's behalf. At that moment, God spoke to Miss Ellington's heart and said, "It's time to tell Marshall." So, she wrote Marshall a letter and explained everything. She even sent him the very first check for a keepsake.

When Marshall received the letter, he picked up the phone and called Miss Ellington, but when she answered, the "Rabbi" was overcome with emotion. He was simply too choked up to say anything. After a few moments of silence Miss Ellington didn't hang up. The Lord had revealed the source of the phone call, so, she said, "Marshall, is that you?"

Finally, Marshall was able to speak. At long last, he was able to offer heartfelt thanks for a gift that meant so much to himself *and* to every single person who has ever been touched by his ministry.

Before she hung up, Miss Ellington said, "Marshall, this was the greatest investment I ever made!"

Without a doubt, Mary Leila Ellington was a shade-tree planter. And God gets the glory!

YOU KNOW SOMEBODY WHO KNOWS SOMEBODY WHO KNOWS SOMEBODY

Do you remember the 1993 movie *Six Degrees of Separation*, starring Stockard Channing and Will Smith? It was based on the research of Stanley Milgram, a Harvard professor of social psychology. Milgram proved that, on average, folks in the United States are only six people away from knowing anyone else. You know somebody who knows somebody who knows somebody . . . and on the average you are only six somebodies away from *anybody*.

Mrs. Ellington did not know it, but she was only two degrees of separation from setting the entire direction of my life. When you plant a shade tree you'll never sit under, you never know who you may be two degrees away from it. So plant something. When you do, you will change the direction of someone's life.

Not everyone can be a legend . . . but everyone can leave a legacy.

CHAPTER 4

THE TREATY OAK OF AUSTIN

Down in Austin, where the Ole Swan grew up, stands a 500-year-old tree like no other. We call her "The Treaty Oak." People who study trees claim she was one of 14 trees that made up the "Council Oaks," a grove of trees where the Tonkawa and Comanche tribes met. Some local folks think the tribes would meet there to make peace.

Another legend claims that tea made from the acorns of the tree mixed with honey would promise safety to the warriors. Still another yarn imagines that Stephen F. Austin, founder of Texas, met with Native Americans there to make peace after an early raid. There are those who claim Sam Houston rested under the tree after Texas threw him out of the governor's office at the beginning of the Civil War. Sam wanted Texas to be a free state rather than a slave state. Other old stories crowd around the trunk of the old tree by the dozens.

In 1989 the old tree gained worldwide fame when a lunatic poisoned it. He used an herbicide so strong it could have killed an entire forest. The whole dad-gum country got mad. The tree got get-well-quick cards. Ross "do you get my drift?" Perot gave a blank check for the recovery of the tree. I like Ross, what a great American! He shows up with me all over the country in my routines. Thank God for his ears.

The Treaty Oak was supposed to croak. But, tree doctors put sugar around its roots, and they sprayed the thing with spring water. To everybody's surprise the tree survived. It's not what it used to be, but it is still there, and it's still alive.

Then came a surprise. In 1997, against all odds, the tree produced another crop of acorns, the first since the poisoning. That event was about as likely as the Texas Aggies loving Bevo, the UT mascot.

Folks gathered the acorns and sent them all over the Lone Star State and beyond. The goal, of course, was to grow new trees and multiply the majestic memory of the Treaty Oak. Now, that old oak will have children and grandchildren trees in many states and several counties.

Every time I go home I think about that old Treaty Oak. Could there be a better example of saving a shade tree so others can it be under it? That tree has taught Swan some life lessons.

WE NEED FORGIVING HEARTS
AND COMPASSIONATE SPIRITS

Some folks are born again and other folks are born against. The latter wake up in a minor key, and if things ever calm down they find a way to stir them up. A friend, describing a testy college president, said, "That man can walk through a room and divide people by just showing up." Some folks bring concord and others bring discord.

Jesus told a story about a man who would not forgive (Matt. 18:21-35). That man, himself a slave, owed "a certain king" a bit of money (think: Fort Knox). But when the man begged the king for forgiveness, the king granted it and wiped away the debts. Whew!

Later, the very same man, the one whose big debts had been wiped away, refused to forgive a fellow slave who owed him a few bucks. When the king got word of what had happened, his highness had good reason to be furious. So the king, who had originally forgiven the slave's debts, changed his mind. The king locked up the unforgiving slave and threw away the key.

Jesus tells you and me that God will do the same thing if we do not forgive. I don't know what that means, but I don't like the sound of God locking me up and throwing away the key. I like to move around more than that.

WE ALL NEED PLACES WHERE
PEACE CAN BE MADE

We all need a Treaty Oak, a place in our hearts where peace can be made. After all, what good does it do us to keep playing the same tapes over and over in our heads?

In Texas there's a ranch that covers 800 square miles. After the old man who founded the ranch died, the family has fought over the land for decades, divided into two feuding branches of the family living in their own ranch houses, arguing over enough land that half of it could be a state in New England. In the middle of drinking, divorce, and dissension, some of the fighting folks have died, and the quarrel was never settled. Now, here is the interesting thing: The only part of that ranch that some of them got was the part that's six feet underground.

If you are in a fight, get to the Treaty Oak. Have a place where you bury the hatchet, make peace, give it up, chill out, and let bygones be bygones. And while you're at it, you might consider that God will lock you up and throw away the key if you cannot forgive. If Jesus forgave you what you *know* you did, you sure as heck had better forgive somebody else what squat they did to you. Or else.

At the Treaty Oak You Find Character That Survives and Multiplies

Will Rogers chuckled, "Folks who fly off the handle at the drop of a hat usually make a bad landing." There's something wonderful about those special folks who live long, enjoy life, and seem at peace. They don't live with grudges, hatreds, animosities, and unsettled disputes. They do what it takes to get things settled, and they are inevitably rewarded for their efforts.

Rev. Harry Blake is pastor of Mt. Canaan Baptist Church in Shreveport, Louisiana. He is an icon of the city. He is an African-American minister. He was the youngest field representative of Rev. Dr. Martin Luther King. Rev. Blake was 25 when in September 1963 the four little girls were killed in a Birmingham church bombing. Like black ministers all over the South, he intended to lead a peaceful march of protest in Shreveport. He asked the police commissioner for permission to march. When no answer came, he called off the march.

The police commissioner had Blake dragged out of his church anyway. Then, two policemen beat him into unconsciousness and left him for dead in the church yard. Harry Blake had done nothing. He was inside his own church. The march had been cancelled.

Now here is the "rest of the story." Later that police commissioner was exposed for corruption. Still later, when the commissioner was dying, he called for one man to come pray for him, and one many only. That man was Rev. Dr. Harry Blake. Blake went to the commissioner's beside and prayed for the man who attempted to have him beaten to death.

Today, Rev. Dr. Blake is a distinguished leader of the National Baptist Convention and a leading (and beloved) citizen in Shreveport. The City Council formally apologized to him for the beating decades before. The haters are mostly gone, and Rev. Blake still leads, preaches, and stands as a living witness to the power of redemptive forgiveness.

Take some advice from Swan. Get over it. Pray for—and with—your enemies. Bless them. Encourage them. Forgive them . . . and get on with life.

> Get over it. Pray for—and with—your enemies. Bless them. Encourage them. Forgive them . . . and get on with life.

A TEST WORTH TAKING

Have you ever tried to decide how much onion you have to peel off to get to the real onion? When I have to peel an onion I can never decide when I get to the real onion. Do I need to take off one more layer? What if someone could peel you down to the real you, the inner you. What would they find there? Anger, lust, revenge, fear, and greed, or peace, purity, forgiveness, and generosity? Somewhere deep within is the core of everyone, the center of the center.

The Ole Swan has a test that reveals that "center-of-the-center" factor. And, it's a test that can be administered in an instant. So here's the test: *How do you act when someone overlooks you, ignores you, and does not recognize you.*

This is a nice, quiet, private test that you can take all of the time. Folks who are sweet on the inside just keep on being sweet. Folks who are bitter on the inside let the bitterness out. Try that quiz. It is revealing.

IT'S GOOD TO HAVE SOME SUGAR
AT THE ROOTS

Now, it probably goes without saying, but I'll say it anyway: I am *not* a tree doctor. But, I do think it's funny how they saved the Treaty Oak by putting sugar around the roots. As it turned out, the best antidote for the herbicide was sugar.

Mayor Bloomberg may not want New York City kids drinking Big Gulps, but there is nothing wrong with having sugar around your roots, at the very center of your being. In Mark 7:20 Jesus makes it clear that what defiles a person comes from deep within the person. What is deep within you?

A number of years ago, a new student arrived in a taxi at Union Seminary in New York City. Noticing a white-haired man in shirtsleeves standing by the door of the dormitory, the student asked rather arrogantly, "Hey, mister, do you work here?" Hearing that the man did, indeed, work at the seminary, the new arrival commanded, "Then you may take my bags up to Room 309." The older man silently picked up the two heavy suitcases and trudged up the three flights of stairs to the door of 309. The student followed, holding only his raincoat and a light briefcase. When the door was opened, the new student casually offered the man who carried his luggage a small coin. The gentleman with the white hair politely thanked the young fellow but declined the tip.

> It is easier to act your way into a new way of feeling than feel your way into a new way of acting.

The following day, the newly arrived student joined the rest of the seminary community in the opening communion service. He was shocked to see that the man he had assumed to be a porter was up on stage, wearing a pulpit robe, and presiding at worship. When he whispered to a neighbor, the young man learned that the white-haired man was the president of Union Seminary, the esteemed and world famous Dr. Henry Sloane Coffin.

Rushing up to President Coffin afterward, the student began to stammer his apologies for so brusquely commanding Dr. Coffin to carry his bags the day before. The renowned Dr. Coffin allowed himself a small smile, and gently answered.

"The Son of Man came not to be served but to serve. We must do likewise," It was the most important lesson that young ministerial student learned during his three years at Union Seminary. Sweet goes all the way to the bone.

BE SWEET

If you want to be a shade that lasts and blesses, get some sugar down at the roots. Artificial sweeteners will not work. See the best in folks, not the worst. Smile at strangers. Throw somebody's paper on their porch during your early morning walks. Pick up the trash from a stranger's yard and never tell anybody you did it. Pay for the folk's coffee in the car behind you at Starbucks. Give your preacher a ten-dollar bill at the church house door. Send somebody a subscription to their favorite magazine, and don't tell them who did it.

It is easier to act your way into a new way of feeling than feel your way into a new way of acting. Act sweet and you will get that way.

CHAPTER 5

PLANTING SHADE TREES WITH DEEP ROOTS

When I was a little boy, I tried on several occasions to see how deep I could dig a hole. I heard that you could dig a hole all the way to China, and I wanted to find out if it was true. Also, I loved to dig up ant beds to look for the queen ant. I never found her. I thought she would be wearing a crown and sit on a throne.

Whether we are young or old, there is always a fascination with how deep things actually are.

How deep would you guess the deepest tree roots can grow? In South Africa near the Echo Caves stands a rare grove of wild fig trees. The entire area yields plenty of mysteries. On the surface the fig trees appear to be average, unexceptional plants. That, however, is only on the surface. Researchers have discovered that the roots of the trees descend 400 feet into the mysterious Echo Caves. These humble fig trees have the deepest known root system on the planet.

The South African fig trees penetrate rock and dirt in an amazing quest for water in a dry land. The roots extend down further than a football field (including both end zones). Such a root system challenges the human imagination. Beyond that, the roots must engage a process called osmosis that carries that water 400 feet upward, fighting against gravity, for the water to reach the tree on top of the ground. This process is as striking as the depth of the roots themselves.

The sweet singer of Israel opened the song book of the Old Testament with the psalm that celebrates a life that is like a tree planted by the rivers of water. Such a tree sends it roots into the abundant moisture that saturates the soil along the banks of a flowing river. The picture is one of abundance and never-ending supply. That kind of resource enriches trees that flourish in every season. The supply beneath them in hidden places mysteriously feeds them from root to branch.

Paul wrote of a similar secret in 2 Corinthians 4:16: "Even though our outer man is perishing our inner man is being renewed day by day beyond all measure." The person in touch with God's hidden inner resources finds a wellspring within that never exhausts the endless resources of God.

The toughest race the Swan knows about is the Australian ultra-marathon. The race takes five days and covers 543.7 miles. The runners are world-class athletes under 30. Many are sponsored by international brands such as Nike. One year, a 61-year-old man, Cliff Young, showed up at the starting place for the race. Everyone assumed he was a spectator until he took a number. After all, Cliff was much older than any of the other runners. And another thing: he didn't have running gear. Amazingly, he was wearing overalls and work boots.

The young racers figured the old geezer lost his mind and would pass out after a mile or two. Cliff Young disagreed. He told them he had grown up on a 2,000-acre

God offers hidden resources that are not even understood by most.

sheep ranch with 2,000 sheep. When a storm came, he had to round the sheep up, often running all night. The runners were not impressed. At least not yet.

The race organizers suggested that participants run 18 hours and sleep 6 hours. But, the rules stated that no one was forced to sleep.

When the race began, the younger runners took off and left Cliff far behind. Yet to the astonishment of the racers the next day he had gained significant ground on the entire field. TV crews followed him, and experts laughed at his peculiar shuffle. No one had told Cliff that he was supposed to sleep! So he ran all night . . . *every night*. By the last night of the five-day race, he led the field. The nation was astounded when the 61-year-old sheep farmer won the race. When he was given the $10,000 prize, he humbly said he did not even know there was a prize, so he gave it away to the other runners.

Cliff Young had deep roots, resources that no one else in the race knew about. A lifetime of discipline and endurance prepared him for that moment. He sent the roots of life deep into those resources, and they sustained him with a breathtaking stability and perseverance. The same can be true in your life as well. Through our Lord Jesus Christ, God offers hidden resources that are not even understood by most. You can sink the roots of your life into those resources through quietness, meditation, prayer and retreat with God.

HOW WATER GETS FROM THE ROOTS TO THE TOP OF THE TREE

Remember the tree with the deepest roots in the world? How does water climb up 400 feet through the roots system to the top of the tree? If you can understand that, it can help you know how God gives His resources to you in mysterious ways.

Eugene Peterson, who translated the famous dynamic equivalent Bible translation *The Message*, believes that everything in nature illustrates something in grace. That is certainly true with trees.

Do you recall studying something in high school called "osmosis"? Please don't get confused. I do *not* mean *The*

Osmonds. They were somebody else. I mean *osmosis.* It's the mysterious way that water moves through trees—and you—from one place to another. Now don't check out on me. My physics professor at Baylor University, Dr. Robert Packard, told us something else about osmosis. Osmosis reflects some particular physical qualities of water that picture some spiritual truths as well.

First, osmosis moves water full of stuff from areas of greater concentration to areas of lesser concentration. When one cell is full of stuff that gives life and the cell right next to it does not have as much stuff, osmosis passes that stuff to the cell next door, the one that needs it. It is the opposite of the "the rich get richer." In osmosis the rich cell gives to the poor cell next door. In fact, the rich cell gives so much that it becomes equal to the cell next to it. There is balance between the two.

Beneath all of that old biology is a wonderful spiritual truth. The resources of God move from God, who has more resources than we can imagine, into our little lives that need them desperately. The same way water moves up a 400-foot root to the top of a tree, God feeds us with resources from His fullness to our emptiness.

Dr. Packard told us something else about osmosis: water attracts other water. This process is called adhesion. Think of adhesive tape wrapped around your ankle. It sticks to itself. Water sticks to itself. Water molecules like other water molecules. The reason water climbs up a 400-foot tree root is its attraction to other water.

Again, there is a wonderful spiritual truth. When the life of Jesus Christ lives in you, it always attracts more of the life of Jesus Christ. The Jesus already in you attracts more of the eternal Christ from beyond you. When you know some of Him, you will always want to know more of Him. The Christ-life always attracts more of the Christ-life.

That reminds me of something else Dr. Packard said about osmosis. He said that water likes to go from bigger places into little places. This is called *capillary action*. Trees have little tubes that go from the bottom to the top of the tree. The closer they are to the top of the tree the smaller they get. Water goes from big places into little places. That is why a paper towel soaks up the cola Swan spills on the floor. When there is a lake of cola on the floor, Lauree likes it when it moves from a big place to a small place, a paper towel.

You are probably ahead of me, but I'll say it anyway. God is in the big place, this entire universe that He created. Astronomers tell us that the universe is 14 billion light years from one end to the other. If you rode a beam of light at 186,000 miles per second, it would take you 14 billion years to get from one side to the other. That's longer than it took Baylor to get a Heisman Trophy winner. That is bigger than big.

Yet the God who created all of that bigness yearns to live in the tiny place we call the human heart. The God who lives *everywhere* wants to come to one little *somewhere*, the inside of you. God always moves from the big place to the little place. He even moved from heaven to a cow stable in Bethlehem. God paints a picture of spiritual life in the world of physical

> The resources of God move from God into our little lives that need them desperately.

life. The way water moves up a tree is the way God moves through your life, from His fullness into your emptiness and from His bigness into your littleness. How does that happen? Corrie ten Boom used to say, "Nestle, don't wrestle." Whatever "it" is, you cannot make "it" happen by yourself. You can, however, be at home with God. John calls that "abiding" in God. The same way rich minerals move from the soil through the roots of a grapevine into the sweet grape is the way God moves His life into you (John 15).

LIFE THAT LASTS

In Norway there is a "Doomsday Seed bank." Some of my distant Scandinavian cousins watch it closely. If you ask me, watching seeds sounds like a pretty boring job. Those seeds don't do anything for hundreds of years except sit there, waiting for doomsday. Since I can't stand being bored, I'm glad to be a spiritual seed *planter*, not a professional seed *watcher*.

Anyway, the seed bank is located on a tiny island 810 miles from the North Pole. It is 360 feet inside a sandstone mountain on a tiny island near the North Pole. Inside that seed bank, nations from all over the world send native seeds of all kinds. In case of a world-wide catastrophe, this place acts like the Noah's Ark of seeds. There will always be seeds to start over again! Why? Because seeds contain a principle of life that lasts.

Biologists believe those seeds could sprout after 20,000 years underground in the middle of nowhere. That life came into those seeds from roots then sunk into the soil and transferred the nourishment from the soil to the seeds. That life will last beyond our imagination.

The God who put life-that-lasts into seeds is the same God who can put life-that-lasts into your heart. That life comes from deep roots sunk into His life through time spent in His word, through prayer, through meditation, and through fellowship with people who do the same thing.

Richard Foster said that the three enemies of the spiritual life are noise, hurry, and crowds. When you turn off the noise, stop the hurry, and get away from the crowds, your spiritual roots can absorb the life-giving nourishment that lasts.

SPIRITUAL ANCESTRY

Have you ever played with ancestry.com on the Internet? You can put the names of a few of your relatives into their website, and it can build a family tree. I put Floyd's name in, along with a few others, and found the roots of the Swanberg family tree.

Did you know that you also have a spiritual family tree? Your roots go all the way back to the eyewitnesses of Jesus' life, the men who wrote the gospels. In fact, one of the 12 apostles, plus Paul, told somebody who told somebody who told somebody all the way down to you. You will not know it until you get to heaven, but your spiritual roots go back to Paul or Peter or Thomas or Matthew or one of the Twelve.

It's fun to know about your physical ancestors, but it's absolutely necessary that you have spiritual ancestors. Your roots can sink into the family of God all the way back to Jesus. Your earthly family may have fallen apart. You may not even know who your biological parents are. That does not matter; what does matter is your spiritual roots.

You can have a family as old as the family of God. I hope you are in that family.

CHAPTER 6

MEMORY TREES

Can a tree swallow a bicycle? A 99-year-old woman claimed to have found a bicycle her son chained to a tree 50 years before. It happened in Vashon, Washington.

Helen Puz became a widow in 1954. At that time, her neighbors gave her a bike out of sympathy. It was a girl's bike. Eventually, her son Don was given the bike but was embarrassed to ride it because it was made for a girl. So, he "accidentally" lost it by chaining it to a tree.

Fast forward half a century. Helen, who was by now nearly 100 years old, was still looking at the bike she had given her son. But oh, how that bike had changed . . . the bike had been "swallowed" by the tree.

What does it look like? Well, the handle bars and the front wheel stick out of one side of the tree and the back wheel sticks out of the other. Meanwhile, the entire bike has been lifted several feet off the ground. Ole Swan figures the story must be true because, hey, that thing had to get inside that tree *somehow*.

For a long time people have known the trees have memories. I once heard of a guy who was a dendrochronologist. I thought that meant he worked in a dentist's office, straightening teeth. Boy, was I ever wrong. Turns out a dendrochronologist is the person who counts tree rings to see how old the trees are. I guess somebody's got to do it. I would rather watch the grass grow.

I was told that tree-ring-counters (my term, not theirs) could tell when it was a wet year and when it was a dry year, when the tree got sick and when the tree got well, when there was fire and when there was flood . . . just by examining the rings inside the tree. I'm 59. I wonder how many rings are inside me.

Trees have their own system to encode memories, and I know some trees that could tell some stories. There was a tree by the driveway in the place I grew up. I used to lock my bicycle chain around that tree. A couple of years ago I drove by the old homeplace. That tree is now 40 inches around. Back then, it was four inches around that tree. When I look at that tree, it is chocked full of memories.

When I was a boy, my motto was, "Have bike will travel." We would have bike races. We would have all-day cap gun wars all over the neighborhood. I remember fixing flats, pumping up leaky tires, oiling the chain, wearing out the brakes. I remember peddling my bike as fast as I could when I saw Floyd come home. So, that little-now-big tree at the house we used to live in holds memories from a half century ago. The tree did not eat my bike, but the tree did eat some wonderful memories.

Do you have a tree that holds any memories for you? I hope you do because memories stick to trees like Velcro. Maybe it's because most trees were there before us, and without us, and will be there after us, and without us. They are just *there*, like silent sentinels in the sun and in the dark, looking down on us and holding our memories in their branches like that tree in Washington holds the bike.

Old mesquite trees in West Texas don't need much of anything, least of all pampering. But most trees do best when they receive some attention. Most trees are healthiest when they're pruned and fertilized. Sometimes trees, like people, even need surgery. Memories are like that. Precious memories need to be examined, pruned, remembered, relished, and recalled. It keeps them fresh and vivid.

Then, there was Grandpa Elof Swanberg's chinaberry tree. He emigrated from Sweden when he was 14. Funny thing, the chinaberry tree was an immigrant, too. Chinaberry trees were natives to the other side of the world, but somebody brought them here in 1830. Once they arrived on good old American soil, those chinaberry multiplied like rabbits. When their berries fall on sidewalks, you can slip on them like ice, but Grandpa didn't have that problem. Birds crowded his trees like LSU fans at a football game.

It just seems funny to me that chinaberry trees immigrated here and Grandpa Swanberg immigrated here. He would sit under the old tree with an old church pew tilted at a 30-degree angle. He cocked his head in an unforgettable pose against the fading blue gray of a Texas late autumn skyscape. Grandpa had lost one arm in a cotton gin accident, so he balanced himself with his remaining arm, waving it in the air to make a point.

> Do you have a tree that holds any memories for you? I hope you do because memories stick to trees like Velcro.

With his lilting Scandinavian accent and his eyes peering at some invisible horizon, he would tell me about the Old Country, sharing memories of a boyhood amidst the fjords and the forests of a world I could not imagine.

Grandpa Swanberg would tell me how he and his sister (both orphans) at age 14 and 16 came to America on the *Lusitania* and landed at Ellis Island. When he arrived, he carried all his earthly possessions in a single trunk, which I now have in my office—what a shade-tree treasure!

I remember the Swedish proverbs my grandfather quoted, sometimes in Swedish and sometimes in English:

"We notice faults of others and easily forget our own."

Man märker andras fel ochglömmer sina egna.

"It is well to learn from the errors of others, since there is not time enough to make all of them by yourself."

Gott lära av andras fel, eftersomman inte hinner begå alla själv."

A faraway tone from somewhere deep inside of Grandpa spoke these words slowly, like savoring the last piece of cornbread in a glass of cornbread and buttermilk.

Grandpa is gone now, as is his son. Sometimes I go back to the bare patch of Texas earth under that tree. The wind blows through its branches. A train whistle dies in the distance. A mockingbird sings. And I hear his voice in the pew, its paint peeling, leaning against the chinaberry tree. And I think to myself how good it is to stand on a spot where somebody once was and hear his voice coming from some thin place between time and forever.

We need to remember chinaberry trees and late fall evenings and accents from somewhere else. Grandpa's roots were as deep as that tree.

My granddad used to take my little hand, and we would walk the fence row. In Texas a farmer has to watch barbed-wire fence rows like a CIA agent watches Iran. Grandpa Swanberg would show me how a hackberry tree had eaten the barbed wire. The rusty ancient wire disappeared into the tree and came out on the other side. Heck, we saw trees that had swallowed tin cans and old farm implements, embracing the lifeless metal inside the living heart of the tree.

In rural Texas old homesteads are hosts to aged, rusting farm equipment: cultivators, plows, even old tractors long put out to pasture. In the evening when shadows grow long and an orange sun shines on the rusty abandoned implements, they almost seem to say something if you listen. They talk about hard honest work. Long weary days. Rest honestly won after harvest is done.

The old tractor over there by the edge of the woods was once the pride and joy of a hardworking farmer, whose face was leathered by the sun. Now he is gone, like Grandpa Swanberg, but he left a plow that once split the soil that grew the grain that fed the people. The farmer, grain, and people are gone, but the tractor and the soil are still there, like the bicycle in the tree, reminding Swan that memories are everywhere if you look for them.

Swan has led folks to the Holy Land. I have walked over rocks, through narrow lanes in Jerusalem, boated across the Sea of Galilee, eaten St. Peter's fish, ridden camels, and bought a forest of olive wood nativity figures. I've got big Josephs, middle sized Josephs, and tiny Josephs. Take your pick.

The Holy Land was once full of trees but is now stripped of trees except for newly planted forests. One tree stands out to me: a sycamore tree in New Testament Jericho. A little man named Zaccheus climbed the tree to see Jesus.

Zach lived on the fringes. He was about as popular as Bernie Madoff. He was a quisling, a collaborator with the enemy, a sell-out Jew who collected taxes for the Roman Empire. Nobody liked him. He even had to watch the Super Bowl by himself. The kids wouldn't come to his house on Halloween. When he walked down the Jericho street, people averted their eyes, or spit, or called him names. He lived in a big house on the hill, but he knew very well that a house is not a home. He knew the price of everything but the value of nothing.

> Memories are everywhere if you look for them.

When Mrs. Zach was in the hospital, Zach tried to bribe the nurses to give her extra attention. One of them told him that his money was no good there; she would get the same treatment as everyone else.

Zach had a stash of cash in his wall safe; the Romans expected him to scam and skim. Just give Rome what Rome wanted, and he could keep the rest. He had a big pad but no guests.

In Jesus' day, important people didn't run; they walked.

For a Jew to run was a sign of indignity, loss of face, lack of decorum. Important people did not run. Yet one day Zach ran. He climbed the sycamore tree. People must have wondered what this self-important Roman official was doing dangling off a limb of a tree. It was like seeing the mayor sitting on a flag pole, or the DA standing on a pickle barrel. It was just not done.

Everybody in town had heard of the stunning rabbi from Nazareth. He was the most looked at person in the Holy Land. Thousands looked at Him daily as He preached and healed. But not everyone looking at Him really saw Him. Zach climbed that tree and not only looked at Jesus, but also saw Him.

When it comes to Jesus, there is a difference between looking and seeing. From his perch on a limb, in the most famous sycamore tree in history, Zach saw Jesus. Jesus then invited Himself to the big house on the hill where there were plenty of seats but no one to sit in them. The guest became the host, and Zach opened the wall safe and threw dirty money all over Jericho. Nobody could believe it.

I wonder how people looked at that sycamore tree after Zach's transformation. Fathers told their sons and grandpas told their granddaughters about the day Zach climbed the tree and the Son of God stopped under the tree. I think somebody probably put a stone on the street by the tree, maybe like the Walk of the Stars in Hollywood: "Jesus Stopped

Here." A hundred years later the new Christians in Jericho would stop and stare and pray and weep and laugh and squint up to the limb where Zach sat. That tree probably became a finger pointing towards the Lamb of God, a sycamore cathedral where holy things had happened. It became the memory tree. Holy recollection happened daily.

One of the last things I like to do on the Holy Land tour is to slip away from the group and go to the grove of olive trees just in front of the Church of All Nations on the Mount of Olives. Some guides think the present trees are the children of the very trees where Jesus prayed. I like to go early in the morning before the tourist buses jam the mountain like metal boxes strung out down the hillside. Here are the trees where Jesus prayed, "Not My will but Thine be done." My salvation hung in the balance under those trees.

The wind whispers through the peculiar iridescence of the leaves, and I can almost hear the words, "Let this cup pass from me." With very little imagination, I can see Jesus asking nine of the Twelve to stay on the edge, three to come into the garden with him, and then he himself went a stone's throw away.

Sometimes we can't take anybody with us when we wrestle with God. I sit there and wonder if I would be one of the nine on the edge or one of the three in the middle or if I would have been there at all. Actually, I was there.

The late Dr. R. G. Lee once asked a little Arab boy to

take him to the top of Calvary. When the great Memphis preacher stood on the summit of Calvary, he got a strange look in his eyes and looked into the eternal distance.

The little Arab boy asked, "Have you been here before, mister?"

Lee answered, "Yes."

"How long ago, mister?"

"Two thousand years ago."

The little boy's eyes got as big as golf balls. Truth be told, every Jesus follower was in that garden and then on that hill. Jesus died on a tree on that hill. The crosses were not smoothed out lumber from a saw mill. They were roughhewn trees with knotholes and splinters and sap and the butts of sawed off limbs. It was a tree, the ultimate memory tree. Were you there?

CHAPTER 7

BONSAI TREES:
IT'S THE LITTLE THINGS
THAT MATTER

I always think of trees as big, old, or useful. One kind of tree, however, isn't any of that. Folks call them *bonsai* trees. The word bonsai comes from a Japanese name for the little pot the miniature trees grow in. These tiny little trees are grown for the joy of those who see them and for the interest of those who cultivate them.

Instead of chain saws and big trucks, you care for bonsai trees with tweezers and little scissors. Miniature bonsais are from one to ten inches tall, little replicas of much larger trees. For Bonsai devotees, the little trees are reminders of a number of virtues and realities.

Some good things are small. In our modern world, big is *really* big. Big houses, big cars, big bank accounts, and big egos seem to dominate everything. Folks think that if it is big, it is better. Bonsai trees remind us that small can be best and little can be beautiful.

Bonsai trees are also an example of proportion. The trees are pruned so that everything grows in proportion to everything else. You don't see a big trunk with tiny leaves; you see tiny leaves on a tiny limb on a tiny trunk.

Life runs off the rails when it gets out of proportion. There are folks with big bank accounts and shrunken hearts, big houses but little homes, big Outlook Express lists with thousands of names but no real friends, big trips with little enjoyment, and big spenders who know the price of everything and the value of nothing.

You can learn another lesson from the bonsai tree: It leaves no trace of the artist. All of the attention focuses on the tree.

Some folks want to focus not on what God has done but upon what *they* have done. They consider themselves to be "artists," creating their own masterpieces along the way, seeking fame, glory, and public acclaim. To do so is a breathtakingly huge mistake. The better way, of course, is to be like a humble Bonsai tree-farmer: put all the focus on the tree.

God remains the center of focus in a healthy heart. You cannot draw attention to yourself and honor God at the same.

Jesus never seemed to be impressed by mere bigness. In fact, when His disciples pointed out the size and the value of the Temple in Jerusalem, He stunned them with the prophecy that not one stone would be left on top of another (Matt. 24:2).

Jesus liked to hang out with little people in little places, not with big shots in big places. You can almost feel His empathy for the nameless, the poor, the unidentified folks who gathered around Him and pleaded for His help. He took a group of backwater little people—Peter, Andrew, James, and John—and gave them to the world forever as His apostles. He pruned them and fertilized them and cared for them and gave them to the ages.

> You cannot draw attention to yourself and honor God at the same time.

Little things have the capacity to blast or to bless. Song of Solomon 2:15 warns against the little foxes that spoil the vines. An ancient vineyard owner went all-out to protect his vineyard. He had made a great investment in digging out the rocks, planting the choicest vine, building a hedge around the vineyard, and setting up a guard tower to watch the vineyard (Isaiah 5). While on the watch for the big threats, he could easily forget the little foxes that could climb through the hedge and eat the tender young vines before they could bear fruit. This is why bonsai trees serve as a warning against those little things that eat away at life.

You'll feel better, be healthier, live longer, and bless more people if you develop a sense of contentment. Some folks wake up every morning with their psychological radar tuned in such a way that they spot the one thing *wrong* in the midst of a thousand things *right*.

I spoke to the wife of an affluent friend who went on and on about the trials of her day. First, she had to get to her personal trainer after her massage and manicure. Then, she had to go all the way across town to Neiman Marcus to pick up a new gown. All these efforts, she complained, just wore her out. I wanted to say, "Lady, would you please listen to yourself?" She was hardly a martyr.

Be content with little things.

RUDENESS DOESN'T PAY

A rude person fouls the air everywhere he goes. On the other hand, a kind person spreads a pleasant spiritual aroma (2 Cor. 2:14).

With that thought in mind, you need to learn something: Everybody is struggling, and I mean everybody. The "little" people are struggling, and so are the "big" people. The rich people have problems just like the poor people. The PhD and the no-D: same thing. They're all wrestling with something that could drag them down at any moment. So, be an encourager. Say a positive word. You never know when it will come back to you.

Just like a kind word can boomerang back (and make your life better), so can an unkind word boomerang (and make your life worse). Rudeness has a way of coming back at you.

The president of the Houston Community College, a huge municipal college with 80,000 students, got onto an elevator and greeted a woman on the elevator. He was black, and she was white. She did not say a word. He greeted her again, and she looked the other way. Finally, he asked her why she would not greet him back.

In a waspish voice she answered, "I don't want to, and I don't have to."

The man got off the elevator and went into the executive suite where his corner office looked out over the city. Shortly, his secretary buzzed in with a résumé in hand. The secretary told him that a woman urgently needed to see him. You are ahead of the story. It was the woman on the elevator.

The college president told the woman, "You will never work for the Houston Community College." She learned a hard lesson about rudeness and kindness. He had shown her the kindness of a greeting while she returned the insult of no answer.

When it comes to kindness and rudeness, there's an immutable law of sowing and reaping. When you sow good things, good things have a way of coming back to you. When you sow bad things, those bad things, like homing pigeons, eventually come to roost. So remember the lesson of the bonsai and be kind in little things.

LITTLE THINGS CAN MAKE A BIG DIFFERENCE, ESPECIALLY WHEN THOSE LITTLE THINGS ARE SMALL ACTS OF KINDNESS

A friend of mine had a careless paperboy. Sometimes the paper was in the street. Sometimes the paper was on top of the house. Sometimes the paper was behind a tree. He never knew where the paper would be.

Then, suddenly, the paper was directly on front of his door every morning. The paper was squarely centered at the threshold of his door as if someone had measured the door and placed the paper precisely at the center. He was sure that the goofy paperboy hadn't suddenly learned how to pitch like Nolan Ryan. He found out that a neighbor he hardly knew put the paper there on his pre-dawn walk every morning.

The neighbor never told him; my friend found out indirectly. The neighbor did little things and didn't tell anybody. Jesus encourages you to be generous, but He doesn't want you to buy a billboard to tell everybody what you're doing.

You will find enormous fulfillment in doing little things for little people that no one ever knows about. Slip an envelope with $20 in it under the door of a homebound

> Small acts of kindness won't bring world peace, but they will change the day for somebody.

widow. When you see a needy kid in line at Wal-Mart, give him a buck to get something and walk away (and while you're walking, don't hug yourself to death). Ask somebody behind you in line at Starbucks what her favorite drink is, quietly buy it for her, and disappear. After you've done a good deed, get out of the picture.

Small acts of kindness won't bring world peace, but they will change the day for somebody. God does not expect you to eradicate world hunger, but He is on the side of those who do little things for little people.

SOMETIMES, THINGS THAT START OUT SMALL DON'T STAY THAT WAY

On February 1, 1845, three men met in a cold dusty room at the tiny capital city of the Republic of Texas, then an independent nation. The town was small, the little capital uninspiring, and the plan so audacious that no one could have taken it very seriously. The men proposed to start a university in a state that didn't have a dozen folks with a college degree. They didn't have any money for the project, no campus, and no faculty.

Today that tiny idea now has 150,000 living graduates, sits on 750 acres, has a student body of 15,000, an endowment of more than a billion dollars, and, as of 2011, a

Heisman Trophy winner. Oh, incidentally, the school I'm talking about is my alma mater, Baylor University.

That cold February day in the tiny capital, R. E. B. Baylor, William Tryon, and James Huckins planted a bonsai tree. That tree has provided shade for thousands of ministers, missionaries, doctors, lawyers, school teachers, accountants, musicians, and folks who have helped carve cities out of the prairie, careers out of nothing, and lives that matter. Those men planted a bonsai tree, and it turned into a giant redwood.

CHAPTER 8

PLANTING SHADE TREES: FIRES, SEEDS, AND MORE TREES

They call them Monterrey pines in California, Jack pines in the north, and Table Mountain pines from Georgia to Pennsylvania. The pine cones on these trees are sealed shut by hardened resin, which forms a prison for the seeds. It takes a forest fire to melt the resin, open the cones, cause the seeds to drop, and create new life.

Without the fire, there is no future. Without the melting, the seeds have no meaning. It takes the flame to create the future. Apart from an occasional fire, there would be no new trees.

Pine trees create a shady canopy for generations. Yet that canopy comes at a cost; the cost is fire. When the Swan thinks of planting shade trees you will never sit under, it reminds me of some great passages of Scripture. Paul wrote in 2 Corinthians 4:17, "This light momentary tribulation is working out an eternal weight of glory beyond all comparison." The phrase from the weight room may sound trite, but it is spiritually true: "No pain, no gain."

DRAG AND LIFT

Yours truly spends a lot of time in airports and on airplanes. I have flown on just about everything that has a propeller or a jet. Big planes and tiny planes, private planes and commercial planes. I have seen them all and then some.

Sometimes, when a plane sits poised at the end of the runway and the flight attendant has told us for the tenth time to power down everything with an on-off switch, the Swan thinks of what is about to happen. The plane has two things going against it when it takes off. Problem #1: Gravity pulls the plane down and wants to keep it on the ground. Problem #2: The air in front of the plane creates something they call "drag," which slows the plane down when it moves forward. Gravity pulls down, and drag slows down.

Yet the very air that creates the drag also makes the plane take off. The wing of a plane is an airfoil that overcomes drag and creates lift. If there were no drag, the plane wouldn't have the air it needed to fly. And Swan would be putting on the brakes at the end of the runway. If you don't believe me, just try flying an airplane in outer space . . . trust me: it doesn't work because there's no air to fly through.

So, if there were no drag, there would be no lift. That is not only a principle of flying; it is also a principle of the spiritual life: The very things that seem to slow us down become the very things that lift us up.

The 26th president climbed up to glory on the very things that would hold him down. As a boy, he suffered asthma of such severity that his family thought he would not live. As a Harvard student, he was examined by the college doctor who told him that he had a heart condition and would have to live a sedate life. He worshipped his father with a total devotion only to see his father die while he was in college.

As a young state legislator in Albany, New York—at the age of 25—he lost both his wife and his mother on the same day, February 14, 1884. He fled to the West, alone, and lived a wild life as a cowboy. But, he was so nearsighted he would be lost without his glasses. Yet that same man charged up San Juan Hill into immortality, served as governor of New York, and became the youngest president of the United States when William McKinley was assassinated. We have a beloved nickname for him because we have affection for him: Teddy. Teddy Roosevelt.

It's appropriate that Teddy Roosevelt's face is carved into the granite of Mount Rushmore because he climbed to the top of his own personal mountain gripping onto one difficulty after another.

At age 25, after the loss of his lovely bride in childbirth,

Theodore Roosevelt wrote in his diary now at Harvard, "The light has gone out in my life forever." He made no more entries into that diary. Yet Roosevelt had not even begun his ascent to the historical greatness he achieved. He reached the heights by using the depths as his foothold.

In Job 36:15 Elihu advises the troubled, tortured Job, who had lost everything, "He delivers the afflicted by their affliction." The very thing that at this moment seems to afflict you is that very thing God can use to move you onward and upward for His purposes.

One of my heroes is Nelson Mandela, the brave leader of South Africa. That man went to jail for 20 years just because he had a darker suntan than some of us and because he wanted all of his people to be free. When his oppressors, the Afrikaners, put him in jail, he used the long sentence to learn the Afrikaner language, the tongue of his jailers. When he was reproached for this, he answered his fellow countrymen, "I might just get out someday and be president." That is exactly what he did.

Mandela used the time in jail, a troubled, tortured time, as a stepping stone to greatness. Incidentally, when Paul was in jail, he used the time to write Philippians, Colossians, Ephesians, and Philemon. He transformed jail time into a time of spiritual advancement, a precious gift for the ages. If Swan were in jail the chapter 1 verse would be, "Get me out!"

LOOK AT THE MOUNTAIN GOAT

Mountain goats amaze me. The Swan has a hard time standing up on snow skies, but mountain goats can stand on a solid rock mountain at a steep angle and stay completely stable. God has given them unusual feet. They have a cloven hoof with toes that spread far apart to give them stability. They have rough pads on the bottom of their feet that act like Velcro on the mountain. Then they have a special claw on the back of their hooves called a "dew claw" that clutches the mountain in an efficient but invisible way. That is why mountain goats can jump 12 feet at a time on the side of a steep mountain. The Swan can jump one foot at a time, on a good day, on level ground.

> God gives you the stability to make stumbling stones stepping stones.

Mountain goats have what it takes to stand in the toughest of places. They use those tough places as a stage to demonstrate their amazing strength and dexterity. The very place that trips other creatures becomes the springboard for their remarkable display of nimbleness.

God did not restrict His mountain-climbing plans to goats! He has the same plan for you. The psalmist exclaimed, "He set my foot upon a rock" (Ps. 40:2). The apostle Paul wrote, "Having done all, stand" (Eph. 6:13). God gives you the stability to make stumbling stones stepping stones. He can use the very thing that might trip you up as a means of elevating you. The God of the goats, the same God who gave them every tool they need to climb, will do the same for you.

Those who plant shade trees for others to sit under have learned how to use adversities as opportunities. No mountain is too steep for them to find a foothold to the next level.

THERE IS A REASON FOR THE RESIN

Lauree likes to collect jewelry. One of her favorites is amber. You would not believe how this semi-precious stone becomes a thing of beauty and value. Amber started out millions of years ago as resin, the gooey stuff that oozes out of trees. When Swan was a little boy climbing trees, it made my hands sticky. I also learned you could put it on your hands to catch a baseball or football better. Old George Brett rubbed it on his bat when he tagged Goose Gossage in the famous 1983 protested game, the "Pine Tar" game. It is sticky stuff. So how could it turn into a beautiful gemstone?

When those old trees died along with the dinosaurs, they got buried under tons of dirt, deeper and deeper. Along with the pressure from the dirt above, things just got hot as the trees sunk farther underground. The combination of the heat and the pressure turned the gooey resin into amber colored stones. Sometimes the resin had trapped an insect or a leaf inside. Those beautiful stones are enhanced in value when they preserve a little piece of life from millions of years ago. It took the heat and the pressure to make the beautiful stone.

God does a similar thing in our lives to create people who can plant shade trees for others to sit under. It takes the heat and pressure of life, with its pitfalls and traps, blindsides and ambushes, astonishments and absurdities, to craft us into the people God wants us to become.

FLIP THE SCRIPT

Peter wrote to the early Christians under persecution, "Dear friends, don't be surprised at the fiery trials you are going through, as if something strange were happening to you" (1 Pet. 4:12 NLT). The Big Fisherman urged the Christ-followers never to imagine that trials and tribulations are foreign to the Christian experience.

For the earliest Christians, life-with-trial was to be expected, while life-without-trial was the exception. The norm was the testing. The expected was the tribulation. The typical was the trial. Someone said of the earliest Christians that they were always in trouble and always hilariously joyful. We, too, should flip the script. We should consider the absence of trial to be the unusual thing and the presence of trial to be the normal thing.

Just as the forest fire releases the seeds from the Monterrey pine—seeds that give birth to more trees—the fires of life release the life of Christ in us in ever deeper and more significant ways.

Christians who have shaken the world often lived in the heat of fire much of their lives. C. H. Spurgeon came to London at 19 years of age, and until he died in 1892 no place could be found that he could not fill. The Metropolitan Tabernacle built to accommodate the crowds that came to hear him preach was filled with 5,000 people every Sunday. No preacher ever planted more shade trees for others to sit under. Many of his sermons, along with his daily devotional book *Morning and Evening*, continue to bless Christians all over the world to this day, 120 years after he went to heaven. Spurgeon planted shade trees all over the world, yet his life was lived in the midst of fire.

When he came to London and became such a preaching phenomenon, many Baptists, Anglicans, and newspapers vilified him mercilessly. On one occasion, gang members cried "Fire!" when he was preaching to a huge throng, and seven people were trampled to death. Spurgeon was so depressed he could not leave his room for days.

His wife Susannah fell ill at the height of his ministry and could not come to hear him preach. He suffered from gout, rheumatism, and Bright's disease, which ultimately took his life. During the last five years of his life he was involved in a nasty denominational controversy that cut his life short. It is safe to say that few years of his unparalleled ministry were without pain. Many consider him the greatest preacher of history after the apostolic times. Yet his life was lived in the fire.

That fire dropped so many seeds. There are 56 volumes of his sermons still in print and now digitized all over the world on the Internet. Spurgeon's College still trains ministers. Thousands of people per year visit his church and his grave in West Norwood Cemetery. No preacher in history still inspires more people in more ways than Spurgeon. No one even comes close. He planted shade trees that will grow until Jesus comes. And he planted them in the midst of fires.

You'll have lots of fires in your own life, and you'll never enjoy them. But when you're walking through the flames, please remember that shade-tree planters have almost always been people who dropped their seeds during the fires of life. Those fires mysteriously opened their lives to the blessings of God in ways we cannot understand. Your own fires will do the same for you.

CHAPTER 9

THE CEDARS OF LEBANON

I've traveled a lot and seen quite a few national monuments: London has Big Ben. Paris enjoys the Eiffel Tower. Rome boasts the Coliseum. Egypt shows you the pyramids. Greece points to the Parthenon on the Acropolis in Athens. Each of these monuments has an interesting story.

The most impressive national monument I have seen, however, is not built of bricks or steel. The Cedars of Lebanon loom over mountains like majestic mirages of a vanished world. They are by far the most frequently mentioned tree in the Bible, with more than 70 citations in the holy text. One of my favorite is Psalm 92:12: "The righteous flourish like the palm tree and grow like a cedar in Lebanon."

When snow falls on the Lebanese mountains, the cedars have the capacity to form a sort of canopy out of their branches that minimizes the weight of the snow on the tree. That is one way they've survived for more than a thousand years. They have learned how to deal with the perennial weight of adversity in the wisest way.

Jesus made it clear for everyone: "In this world you will have tribulation" (John 16:33). Some folks spend their lives trying to run away from trouble and avoiding difficulty. God does not promise you that you can outrun tribulation. No amount of success insulates you from tribulation.

Joseph P. Kennedy, the famous patriarch of the Kennedy clan, lived a vivid of life of success in business, Hollywood, government service, and investing. Many envied his homes in Hyannis Port and Palm Springs. He lived a life of luxury and achievement. Yet he endured more heartbreaks than most.

> I need wisdom to face the inevitable tribulations of life. God promises that.

Kennedy's oldest son Joe died in World War II. Two of his sons were assassinated, and one of his daughters lived with the results of a botched lobotomy that was intended to help her mental condition but made it much worse. As an old man, he suffered a stroke and spent his last years staring at television day and night as an obsession.

Julia Child entertained generations of Americans with her screechy voice and television cooking antics. An awkward, ungainly woman who lacked any natural grace, she seemed to be a guest in every kitchen. Yet her life was filled with tribulation.

Child spent most of her life alienated from her opinionated father whom she could never please; she had no idea what she would do with her life until she was 50 years old; she faced discrimination in French cooking schools because she was a woman; she endured the long decline of her beloved husband Paul; she feuded with the co-authors of her famous cookbook, and she died alone with no family member present.

From outward appearances, both Joe Kennedy and Julia Child lived glamorous lives. By the world's standards, they had it made. But their inner lives were far from glamorous and far from peaceful. Kennedy was a confessing Catholic, and Child had no faith at all, but they did share one thing in common: each endured a lifetime of tribulation.

I have seen enough to know that I need wisdom to face the inevitable tribulations of life. God promises that.

James, the younger half-brother of Jesus, wrote one of the striking biblical promises: "If anyone lacks wisdom, let him ask of God, who gives generously and does not upbraid" (James 1:5). Wisdom is God's viewpoint on your situation. God will give it to you when you ask Him for it, and He will never make you feel stupid. He does not throw your need for wisdom back in your face.

I want to be as wise as the cedar. I want to know how to take the snows of life that fall on me—and they will—and I want to form a canopy of God's grace that can stand up under the weight of the deepest snow.

CEDARS LAST BECAUSE THEY HAVE QUALITIES THAT ENDURE

The wood from the Cedars of Lebanon was the most highly valued building material in the ancient world. Solomon used it in his Temple, and kings used it in their palaces. It was beautiful, hard, and resisted insects. It gave off a wonderful fragrance. You could build with it, live with it, and count on it to last. Lebanese cedar was hardy, appealing, and fragrant.

The older I get, the more I think about the way people build lives. Jesus ended his Sermon on the Mount with a story about two builders. One built his own residence on the dried river bed that the Jews called a wadi. Out in West Texas we call it an arroyo. For most of the year these dried up riverbeds look as hard as asphalt. But looks are deceptive. When the biggest rain of the year comes, these riverbeds turn into foaming monsters, sweeping everything away in their path. What looks durable is not.

On the other hand, Jesus commended the man who dug down deep and did the muscle-straining, bone-jarring work of reaching bedrock. When water rained on the roof, howled against the walls, and rose up to eat the foundation, the house stood. The wise man's house had what it took to withstand the storm.

On July 28, 2009, a thirteen-story high rise in Shanghai fell over like a Lego project. The building was brand-spanking new. Every condo in it had been sold. People were about to move in. The thing snapped at the foundation, and fell over in one piece. One minute it was vertical, and the next it was horizontal. Now, the Swan is no structural engineer, but I can tell you one thing: whoever built that building didn't pay enough attention to the foundation.

If nobody gets hurt, we can chuckle when a building takes a tumble. But there is nothing funny about a life that suddenly falls apart.

When a building loses its value, repairs can be made or insurance can be collected. But with human lives, it's seldom that simple. When a person begins to self-destruct, the results can be long-lasting and tragic. Still, buildings and lives do have one thing in common: When they collapse there's almost always a foundation problem.

> When buildings or lives collapse there's almost always a foundation problem.

Folks who look solid on the outside may be caving on the inside. It is like seeing a falling star. The moment you see a falling star, you can say to yourself, "That never really was a star. If it had been a star, it would not have fallen."

The very first Psalm expresses the theme of all 150 Psalms. Psalm 1 teaches us that a godly person is "like a tree planted by the rivers of water." Down in Austin where I grew up, the sturdiest, oldest, and healthiest trees grow along the banks of the Colorado River. They can send deep roots into the fertile riverbed soil. What's more, in a river bottom, those trees can drink from an abundance of water that runs from the Hill Country into the Colorado River basin.

Not far away, in drier country, trees are stunted, and they often succumb to the blistering Texas heat. The trees near the Colorado River, however, can last for centuries because their roots drink from hidden resources that never dissipate.

The ancients built things with cedar wood because they knew that cedar lasts. So, when God tells the Swan to imitate a tree, I think He intends for me to live in a way that mirrors some of those great cedar trees planted by the water. Those cedars are durable, stable, and rooted.

CEDARS EXUDE A FRAGRANCE BECAUSE OF THE BALSAM THAT COMES FROM WITHIN

To walk in a cedar forest feels like walking into the perfume department at Macy's, except the aroma is more natural. When you cut the cedar it bleeds balsam, and the fragrance makes the cedar forest a delight. Effortlessly the cedar creates a pleasant aroma. The apostle Paul speaks of the aroma we leave when we walk with Christ (2 Cor. 2:16).

Of all the senses, the sense of smell is the most discriminating. You can taste four basic things, but you can smell thousands of things. When you return to a place you haven't visited in a while, the thing that reminds you of that place is the way the place smells. Of all the senses, the most detailed and discriminating is the sense of smell. You can smell more different kinds of fragrances than you can taste flavors, hear sounds, see colors, or feel with the sense of touch.

Have you not been around a Christian who made you think, "What a sweet atmosphere she creates everywhere she goes?" You can't put your finger on it, but there is just something that is in the air when you're around that person. There's a sense of calm, a sense of dignity, a kindness, a grace, a forbearance, and quite a few other positive traits that you can't exactly describe.

Have you ever met someone whom you could identify as a Christian, even before that person told you that he followed Jesus? When you discover some people are Christians, you aren't surprised at all. There's just something about the "atmosphere" those folks create.

Cedars create a sweet fragrance in the forest, and joyful Christians create an atmosphere wherever they go. You cannot put your finger on it, define it, invent it, or imitate it. It is the fragrance of Christ.

Ole Swan wants to imitate a cedar in the fragrance of my life. In a church, at an airport counter when the plane is late, in a hotel hallway greeting the maid, at home, at play, or just in the grocery store looking for Del Monte green beans or potato chips, I want to have that sweet atmosphere that people can't quite put their finger on, even though they know it's there.

Cedars Are Used for Building

Phoenicians, Greeks, Egyptians, and Hebrews all used cedar for building. Solomon most famously used cedar in the Temple (1 Kings 6). The most arresting and costly material in the Temple was the cedar wood imported from Lebanon. Its weight, density, resistance to insects, and abiding quality made cedar the best wood to build with. You could count on it to last the ages.

I have been blessed to study all sorts of folks in churches and secular settings. I speak at 170 events a year, and I've found that you can divide folks into many categories: rich and poor, black and white, educated and uneducated, clergy and laity, labor and management, and a whole lot more. I have noticed that one of the most important divisions is between people who are *constructive* and people who are *destructive*. Some folks build up and some folks just demolish what others have built.

The Bible uses the word, "edify," which literally means "build up." In every encounter, conversation, email, text, or tweet, you are either saying something that builds someone up or something that chips away at them, discourages them, and depresses them. To imitate a cedar means to do and say things that build people up.

Why don't you try it for a day? It is hard by the yard, but a cinch by the inch. For one day, discipline your speech to build people up in every encounter. Be positive. Pay compliments. Encourage. Edify. Smile. You will be astonished at the things that happen across one day of total commitment to be like a cedar, always building.

Because the Hebrews of the Old Testament came from a distant land, they found cedars to be exotic and strange. When they built their Temple, the Hebrews needed help from beyond themselves. That help came in the form of a tree. Yet that tree had to be cut in order to perfume the air with its appealing fragrance. That whole story reminds me of another story.

I needed help from beyond myself. I needed someone to come from somewhere else to help me build my life. That someone had to die on a tree of wood, a rugged Cross. Yet He could not help me until He was cut with the nails of Calvary. I guess He was like a cedar tree more than any person who ever lived.

CHAPTER 10

PUTTING DOWN ROOTS:
THE BANYAN TREE

The banyan tree is the national tree of India. Among other fascinating characteristics, this legendary tree puts down aerial prop roots. That sounds like some kind of airplane, but this prop doesn't propel anything; it's just part of a most amazing tree.

As the branches of a banyan tree grow out from the original trunk, they send new roots straight down from the limb to the ground. Those ground-grabbing roots act as props for an ever-expanding network of branches.

Older banyan trees can spread out over an enormous area by using their prop roots to hold up hundreds of branches. What you wind up with is one tree with a whole lot of trunks holding up a network of limbs that grow farther and farther away from the original trunk. It reminds the Swan of a tree opening up franchises.

Buddha was sitting under a banyan tree when he got enlightened. Swan was looking at a mesquite tree when he got enlightened. Buddha sits around in lots of temples while people adore him. Swan sits around on a lot of airplanes while people ignore him. Where did I go wrong?

I did, however, learn some *serious* lessons from the banyan tree. The banyan lasts because it puts down lots of roots. And, the wider you reach in life, the more roots you need. When your life is stretched out, you need a few aerial prop roots for supports.

Some folks add more and more branches to their lives but don't support the larger branches with new roots. This leads to a collapse. So here's a lesson that I hope you won't forget: for everything you add, something should be taken away.

No mortal should keep adding more engagements, more phone calls, more papers, more hobbies, or more travel without taking something away. When you put something else on top, another thing has to come off the bottom. Even a tree can get into trouble when it does not have enough roots to nourish its branches.

It may seem like a contradiction, but the further you reach out, the more roots you need to put down. And, you shouldn't let your branches outgrow your root system. Just a little observation should make that clear.

> The wider you reach in life, the more roots you need.

Your roots nourish you, but life has a way of sapping your strength and draining your emotional resources. You may start the day brimful of spiritual energy, dynamism, go-power, zip, get-up-and-go and a five-hour energy drink. You are a bag of chips and all of that.

But then, it happens: A negative person drains you in a meeting. Or a critical person punches a hole in your energy. Or a needy person refuses to take care of himself and saps you of your own psychological resilience.

People will flat wear you out. That's life. And, that's why you need to put down more roots, like the banyan tree. Whenever you feel the life of the Spirit ebbing away from you, put down another root. Even Jesus had to do this. After He had healed a whole hospital full of folks in Capernaum, He got up in the dark the next day and put down some roots, some *spiritual* roots (Mark 1:35-37). In the quiet stillness of the predawn desert He had to send down some aerial branches. When He had gone deeper, Jesus could go wider, even into the other surrounding towns. The Son of God didn't try to get more *extensive* without getting more *intensive*. He knew He needed to sink more spiritual roots.

You Have to Guard Your Center When You Add More at the Circumference

As a kid, I watched some *gigantic* epic movies. They had huge sets; they had thousands of extras, and they lasted half a day at the theater. In one of those epics there was a chariot race. On those old chariots, the hub of the wheel was wooden and the axle was wooden, too. Wood rubbed furiously on wood. If the axle was not greased, the wood of the axle created friction with the wood of the hub, and you guessed it: a fire started.

Now, you don't have to be a safety engineer to figure that it's not good when you have a fire in the middle of your wheel. The fire at the center spreads outward along the wooden spokes until the outer circumference of the whole wheel is burning like a Roman candle.

When your hub, spokes, and wheel are on fire, you're not gonna finish the race. If the charioteer failed to guard the center, the whole chariot was destined for the ash heap of history. And when I say "ash heap," I mean it literally.

The banyan tree guards the center. It will not send out longer shoots without more and deeper roots. The roots center the tree, nourish the tree, and support the tree. When you add more and more to the circumference of life without guarding the hub of life, you are likely to face a fire at the center that will spread to the circumference.

Life has some boundaries. Days are 24 hours, and you cannot add another hour to the day. Warren Buffet and Bill Gates cannot. Superman and Spiderman cannot. At some point in life there has to be an exchange. When you take on one more commitment, you should give up another commitment. And, the more commitments you take on, the more roots you need.

ROOTS HOLD YOU UP

The banyan tree can extend its reach because its roots hold it up. The banyan taps invisible resources underground where its many roots cleave to the soil, grip the sub-surface, and anchor the tree. The roots of banyan trees do not grow as deep as the tree is tall. The roots do, however, grow as far out as the farthest reaching branch. People who study trees call that the "drip line."

Wherever you see the farthest reaching branch of a tree, straight down underground is a root that goes out that far. The stability of the tree depends on this foundation, the stretch of the roots as far as the branches extend outward.

A medical doctor, Richard Swenson, wrote an insightful book called *Margin: Restoring Emotional, Physical, Financial and Time Reserves to Overloaded Lives*. The good doctor presents a striking case for how overstretched we are in the most important aspects of our lives. We live at 110% of capacity and then wonder why our lives are not working. Dr. Swenson asks us to slow down, restore balance, and build reserves in every dimension of our lives. The banyan tree thrives because it has a reserve of roots, more than enough to support each branch.

If you're too busy for your own good, even doing good things can flat wear you out. The great devotional writer Oswald Chambers warns about spiritual exhaustion:

> *Exhaustion means that vital forces are worn right out. Spiritual exhaustion never comes through sin but through service and whether or not you are exhausted will depend on where you get you supplies . . . . Be careful where you get your supply or before long you will be utterly exhausted.*

Are you running on fumes? Has the indicator light on the dashboard of your life started flashing empty? Are you rolling to stop because you're flat out of gas? Learn the lesson of the banyan tree and put down some more roots. And, where can you go for nourishment? Well, the best place to start is with the One who never lacks food.

After Jesus fed the 5,000, He explained the higher truth of that

> If you're too busy for your own good, even doing good things can flat wear you out.

physical miracle. He told the seeking crowd, "I am the bread of life" (John 6:35). The source of spiritual energy is the Lord Jesus Christ Himself. If you feed on Him, He will give you spiritual strength that can come from no other source. He is the inexhaustible Person. Everyone else you lean on will eventually run out of the stuff you need. Or they won't be available when you need them.

Mere humans are easily exhausted. Yet when you feed on the Person and words of Jesus you are feeding on a resource that only grows stronger the longer you feed on Him.

THINK ABOUT GOD

The missionary mystic Frank C. Laubach worked in the Philippines and invented a literacy program that has helped millions. He had one driving goal: to think about the Lord all of the time regardless of what else he happened to be doing. He was obsessed with the reality that you can be doing *anything* on the one hand while, on the other hand, having the Lord in your mind. He called it a "game with minutes" and challenged us to begin by thinking of God least one second out of every minute, and then moving upward from there.

Laubach reached a place where he could be thinking of God while typing, teaching, walking, working, or just about anything else he was doing. The approach to life can be very helpful because it challenges you to focus on what's really important. Laubach got *very* good at it. He said, "Each time we try to do better until at last we may be able to remember God as high as 90% of the whole day."

Now, you may think that it is too hard of a challenge to think about God one second out of every minute and then grow from there. Well, let the Ole Swan give you some advice: halitosis is better than no breath at all. If you don't have any plan for thinking about God, you won't think about Him. Just dealing with the dry cleaners, the cable company, the airline counter, and the crazy drivers, will keep you from thinking about God. They will probably make you think more about the devil.

Frank Laubach gives you a plan and a testimony from one who learned how to feed on God all of the time, every day, regardless of what he was doing. Frank became a spiritual banyan tree. You can, too.

Put Down Some Roots, and Don't Go Solo

Somehow the banyan tree recognizes that nothing of significance is done solo. When the banyan tree has sent out branches in every direction and supported its many extra prop roots, the center of the tree often disappears. It did what it could; it started the tree. It gave birth to the life that was there. The time comes when the old trunk disintegrates. The new roots going straight down to the fertile earth become the sustainers of the tree.

Sometimes, heroic discoveries are made alone. You can think of Lister and sanitation, Salk and the polio vaccine, or Hemingway and literature as examples of great things done alone. Yet in every one of those instances, others had to forward the discovery, give the shots, distribute the vaccine, or print the books. Great things that last never happen solo and never happen in a single lifetime. You have to send down new shoots.

There can never be fresh shoots without old roots. If you want life to flourish and bless others, you must always be putting down new roots. The old Quaker philosopher Elton Trueblood recognized a truth about American life. Best Ole Swan can remember, he said that you cannot have the *fruit* of Christianity without the *root* of Christianity. Wow! Was he ever right or was he ever right?

Our secular society wants respect, peace, courtesy, productivity, meaning, and a whole lot of other stuff. Yet we live in what Trueblood called "a cut flower society." We want the fruit without the roots.

Now, even *I* realize that artificial plants don't grow real fruit. Our culture wants the fruit, but the only way to get real fruit is with Christian roots. If we do not have the roots, we cannot have the fruit.

Culture is a mighty big thing. Talking about culture is like the blind man trying to decide where to wash the elephant.

But this much, I do know: You cannot change all of your culture, but you can change your own personal culture. So imitate the banyan tree and put down some new roots.

A Note to Readers

Chapters 11-19 focus on the message of Jeremiah 32. Jeremiah was a great shade-tree planter, and you can be one, too. Here's how:

5 ESSENTIAL ELEMENTS OF A SHADE-TREE PLANTER

SENSITIVITY

You must be sensitive to God's voice;

SURRENDER

You must surrender to God's calling;

SILVER

You must be willing to invest your time,
your talents, and your money;

SIGHT

You must have a vision of the future,
a mental image of God's plan for your unique gift
or your particular contribution;

SIGNATURE

When the time for action comes, you must be willing
to sign your name and seal your pledge.

CHAPTER 11

SENSITIVITY

Sensitivity characterizes every living thing. One of the marks of anything that lives is sensitivity. Along with respiration, growth, and reproduction, sensitivity defines life. A rock is not sensitive. You are. Psychologists have measured the thresholds of maximum human sensitivity. The most sensitive humans can:

- See a candle 30 miles away on a perfectly clear night.

- Hear the tick of a watch under quiet conditions at 20 feet.

- Taste one teaspoon of sugar in two gallons of water.

- Smell one drop of perfume sprayed into the air in a six-room apartment.

- Feel the wing of a fly falling on your cheek from one centimeter.

Now, I cannot do any of those things. I am too blind, too deaf, can't smell, can't feel a fly's wing, and don't want to anyway. Yet psychologists say that the most sensitive people can do all five things above.

I have never found, however, a scale for spiritual sensitivity. How do you measure somebody's sensitivity to the Spirit of God, to the quiet whispers that we only hear somewhere inside? Jeremiah the Old Testament prophet must have ranked high on God's spiritual sensitivity scale. He could hear the voice of God in the biggest messes when nobody else could hear it at all.

About 2,600 years ago, Jeremiah found himself in a bad situation. He was in jail. The king was mad at him. His country was being invaded by the fiercest army in the world. Yet in the middle of all that mess, the Bible tells us that "the word of the Lord came to Jeremiah" (Jer. 32:1). Now, I know what you are thinking. We have all known nutcases who claim to be hearing from God. Some people just like to be odd for God.

When I was in seminary, one student claimed that God told him to jump off the roof of the men's dorm. He did. He broke his head. Jeremiah was different from the nut cases. What God told Jeremiah is in the Holy Bible, and it also really happened. That's not the same as jumping off the dormitory roof.

It's interesting what God told Jeremiah to do. God told him to buy a piece of real estate in a doomed city.

Jeremiah's cousin Hanamel came to him with a sad story (Jer. 32:7). Hanamel was ready to sell the family farm that sat right in the path of the invading Babylonian (Iraqi) army. When you look at an Iraqi today, you see a descendant of the Babylonians. Evidently Hanamel did not know the first three laws of real estate: location, location, location.

In the Old Testament the land belonged to God, but God had given the land forever to families. A member of the family had a sacred obligation to bail out the kinfolks if the kinfolks were about to lose the land (Lev. 25:25-28). It was sort of a brother-in-law deal. Got to help them out; God love 'em.

What is more, God told Jeremiah in advance that cousin Hanamel was going to show up at Jeremiah's doorstep with a sob story. Sure enough, Cuz showed up, deed in hand, and begged Jeremiah to bail out the family farm. Hanamel had no confidence in the future. He was ready to fly out on the first jet from Jerusalem to an all-inclusive resort. He wanted to bail out on the future.

The easiest thing is always to bail out. People bail out of marriages when they get rocky, churches when they don't like a few of the sermons, and degree plans when they have to pull a few all-night cramming sessions. But here's a word of warning: *Nothing of significance ever happens for people who bail out.* When you bail you fail. We have a gospel not just of a good beginning, but of a faithful ending. When the going gets tough, God depends on folks who will not bail out on the future.

Jeremiah believed in the future of God's people in that very place, even though Jerusalem would be invaded, the people carried off to a refugee camp in Iraq, and everybody would be in a funk for 70 years.

There is a city in Arizona named Surprise, Arizona. The town was founded in 1938 by Flora Mae Statler. She named the town "Surprise" because she said she would be surprised if it ever amounted to much. Little did she know. The population was 30,000 in 2000 and 117,000 in 2010! That was a growth rate of 281% in a decade. Flora Mae would be surprised about what has happened to Surprise.

Surprise is in the desert, yet Surprise surprised everybody. Jeremiah could have well named the family farm "Surprise, Israel." Everybody except Jeremiah would have been surprised to find out what God was about to do with the old family farm. That farm became a symbol of God's surprise for His chosen people. Surprise, surprise. Seventy years later God's people would come back, build houses, raise families, plant vineyards, and turn a conquered, desolate nation into God's Holy Land.

Jeremiah was sensitive enough to hear the voice of God when it told him to invest in God's future surprise. Richard Foster reminds us that we can never hear God unless we stop the noise, slow down the hurry, and get away from the crowds.

If you want to be sensitive to God's voice, turn off the noisy stuff, slow down, and get alone. God speaks to those willing to do just that.

When was the last time you just shut it all down, sat still, and did not mind being alone in the quietness? When that happens, God can speak in His mysterious "still small voice" (1 Kings 19:12). Those who get still enough to listen hear what others do not hear, something so quiet and inward that only God can speak in that place.

Find your place. It may be a room in your house, a corner in your yard, or even 15 minutes in your car in the parking garage at work before you get out. One expert in spiritual formation at a famous seminary parked her car every morning where she could look at the school. Then, she sat in silence praying for her day before she went into her office.

Find the place and God will honor your search.

CHAPTER 12

SURRENDER

Beyond his sensitivity, Jeremiah demonstrated surrender. Surrender makes us vulnerable. Surrender runs a risk. Surrender brings up images that we do not normally associate with the successful life in contemporary American culture.

In 1904 William Borden graduated from a Chicago high school. As heir to the Borden family fortune, he was already wealthy. For his high school graduation present, his parents gave the 16-year-old Borden a trip around the world. As the young man traveled through Asia, the Middle East, and Europe, he felt a growing burden for the world's hurting people. Finally, Bill Borden wrote home about his "desire to be a missionary."

One friend expressed disbelief that Bill was "throwing himself away as a missionary." In response, Borden wrote two words in the back of his Bible: "No reserves." Even though young Borden was wealthy, he arrived on the campus of Yale University in 1905 trying to look like just one more freshman. Very quickly, however, Borden's classmates noticed something unusual about him, and it wasn't that he had lots of money. One of them wrote: "He came to college far ahead, spiritually, of any of us. He had already given his heart in full surrender to Christ and had really done it. We who were his classmates learned to lean on him and find in him a strength that was solid as a rock, just because of this settled purpose and consecration."

During his college years, Bill Borden made an entry in his personal journal that defined what his classmates were seeing in him. That entry said simply: "Say 'no' to self and 'yes' to Jesus every time."

Borden's first disappointment at Yale came when the university president spoke in a convocation about the students' need of "having a fixed purpose." After that speech, Borden wrote: "He neglected to say what our purpose should be, and where we should get the ability to persevere and the strength to resist temptations." Surveying the Yale faculty and much of the student body, Borden lamented what he saw as the end result of an empty, humanistic philosophy: moral weakness and sin-ruined lives.

During his first semester at Yale, Borden started something that would transform campus life. One of his friends described how it began: "It was well on in the first term when Bill and I began to pray together in the morning before breakfast. I cannot say positively whose suggestion it was, but

I feel sure it must have originated with Bill. We had been meeting only a short time when a third student joined us and soon after a fourth. The time was spent in prayer after a brief reading of Scripture. Bill's handling of Scripture was helpful. . . . He would read to us from the Bible, show us something that God had promised, and then proceed to claim the promise with assurance."

Borden's small, early-morning prayer group gave birth to a movement that soon spread across the campus. By the end of his first year, 150 freshman were meeting weekly for Bible study and prayer. By the time Bill Borden was a senior, 1,000 of Yale's 1,300 students were meeting in such groups.

Borden made it his habit to seek out the most "incorrigible" students and try to bring them to salvation. A friend observed, "In his sophomore year we organized Bible study groups and divided up the class of 300 or more, each man interested taking a certain number, so that all might, if possible, be reached. The names were gone over one by one, and the question asked, 'Who will take this person?' When it came to someone thought to be a hard proposition, there would be an ominous pause. Nobody wanted the responsibility. Then Bill's voice would be heard, 'Put him down to me.'"

Borden's outreach was not confined to the Yale campus. He cared about widows and orphans and the disabled. He rescued drunks from the streets of New Haven. To try to rehabilitate them, he founded the Yale Hope Mission. One of Bill

Borden's friends wrote that he "might often be found in the lower parts of the city at night, on the street, in a cheap lodging house or some restaurant to which he had taken a poor hungry fellow to feed him, seeking to lead men to Christ."

Borden's missionary call narrowed to the Muslim Kansu people in China. Once he fixed his eyes on that goal, Borden never wavered. He also challenged his classmates to consider missionary service. One of them said of him: "He certainly was one of the strongest characters I have ever known, and he put backbone into the rest of us at college. There was real iron in him, and I always felt he was of the stuff martyrs were made of, and heroic missionaries of more modern times."

Although he was a millionaire, Bill seemed to "realize always that he must be about his Father's business, and not wasting time in the pursuit of amusement." Although Borden refused to join a fraternity, "he did more with his classmates in his senior year than ever before." He presided over the huge student missionary conference held at Yale and served as president of the honor society Phi Beta Kappa.

Upon graduation from Yale, Borden turned down some high-paying job offers. In his Bible, he wrote two more words: "No retreats." William Borden went on to do graduate work at Princeton Seminary in New Jersey. When he finished his studies at Princeton, he sailed for China. Because he was hoping to work with Muslims, he stopped first in Egypt to study Arabic. While there, he contracted spinal meningitis.

Within a month, 25-year-old William Borden was dead.

When the news of William Whiting Borden's death was cabled back to the U.S., the story was carried by nearly every American newspaper. "A wave of sorrow went round the world . . . Borden not only gave (away) his wealth, but himself, in a way so joyous and natural that it (seemed) a privilege rather than a sacrifice," wrote Mary Taylor in her introduction to his biography.

Was Borden's untimely death a waste? Not from God's perspective. Prior to his death, Borden had written two more words in his Bible. Underneath the words "No reserves" and "No retreats," he had written: "No regrets."

No reserve, no retreat, and no regrets. Years earlier Jeremiah could have written the same thing about his decision to buy a plot of land in a condemned city. The Ole Swan has known more than a few people who, at the end, had real reservations about what they had not surrendered and real concerns about the good things they'd retreated from. Please don't make that mistake. Plant some shade trees for others to sit under, and you can say the same thing Will Borden did. His story is a shade tree all by itself.

CHAPTER 13

SILVER

S ome folks seem to think they can take it with them.

A Carson City, Nevada, recluse whose body was found in his home at least a month after he died left only $200 in his bank account. But as Walter Samaszko Jr.'s house was being cleared for sale, officials made a surprise discovery: gold bars and coins valued at $7 million.

"Nobody had any clue he was hoarding the gold," Carson City Clerk-Recorder Alan Glover told the *Las Vegas Sun,* adding it was found stored in boxes in the house and garage. Neighbors told authorities they knew little about Samaszko other than he was quiet and not a problem.

The 69-year-old Samaszko was found dead in his home in late June after neighbors called authorities. He had been dead of heart problems for at least a month, according to the coroner. He had lived in the house since the 1960s, and his mother lived with him until her death in 1992.

Mr. Samaszko left no will and had no apparent close relatives. But using a list of those who attended the mother's funeral, Glover's office tracked down Arlene Magdanz, a first cousin in San Rafael, California, the *Sun* reported. A recording said her phone number had been disconnected.

"Our goal is to get the most money for the heir," Glover said.

The gold coins had been minted as early as the 1840s in such countries as Mexico, England, Austria, and South Africa, he said.

Based on just the weight of the gold alone, Glover estimates their worth at $7 million. Because some of the coins appear to be collector's items, the value could go much higher, he said.

I guess Mr. Samaszko thought he could take it with him, or at least hold on to it until he was at the door to the life beyond. Jeremiah did not make that mistake. When his brother Hanani came to him pleading that Jeremiah buy the family farm as an act of hope, Jeremiah measured out 1.5 years of a working man's salary to pay for the real estate (Jer. 32:9-10). Jeremiah not only paid for the real estate about to be appropriated by the invading enemy Babylonians, but he also did it in a very public way. There were witnesses aplenty when he signed the deed (v. 10).

Now get this: Jeremiah not only bought the land, but he bought it when he was in jail. Not many prisoners buy a doomed piece of land while they are still locked up. All of it was an act of hope that the people of God would one day return and resume life in that very place after their captivity (32:15). Jeremiah became one of the great shade-tree planters of all time.

Jeremiah recognized that it took silver to buy the future. I am amazed how many people get teary-eyed about all God might do for somebody else in the future until they find out it will cost them their silver. When that happens, they get stone-cold sober and speak great platitudes about being careful with their silver. The most sensitive nerve in the human anatomy is the nerve between the pocket book and the heart. Touch some folks there, and you will find out you really touched a nerve.

You see, money is liquid life. You work, and someone gives you money for your work. That is liquid life, the distilled essence of your energy and training and labor. What you do with that liquid life tells a great deal about you. Jeremiah planted a shade tree and did so in a way that everyone could see. Jeremiah intended to invest in the future of children who were not even yet born. He took his own stuff, bought a piece of land, and set it aside as a symbol of hope for children who would come back to that land 70 years later.

Police arrested a Texas woman after they pulled her over for driving erratically and found an eight-month-old baby sleeping under a pile of trash in her back seat.

The police approached her vehicle around 11 p.m. after the woman stopped in the middle of a roadway.

During questioning, she admitted to police that she had consumed a beer and taken Prozac and Xanax, drugs prescribed for depression and anxiety that have serious side effects when mixed with alcohol.

Police conducted a field sobriety test, which she failed, and then searched her car.

That's when they found her eight-month-old baby sleeping in the backseat under a pile of trash, several boxes of clothes, and a skateboard. The child was strapped into a car seat. The woman had buried her child under a pile of stuff.

Most of us could never imagine doing what that troubled mother did. At least, we can't imagine doing it *literally*. But we may do it symbolically. When we take the stuff of life that God gives us and never give a thought about planting it into somebody's life, we may bury someone's future under our stuff.

Sometimes it helps to get out of the theoretical into the specific. What if you imagined a child you could help sitting in the backseat of your car? You could drive the child toward a future of significance, or you could throw your stuff into the backseat and smother the child's chances underneath a pile of possessions the kid couldn't even use. I cannot get the image of that out of my mind. A baby covered up with somebody else's stuff. It's tragic.

MY FATHER'S QUESTION

During the last years of his life, my father's mind began to slip away. Gradually, Floyd Leon lost his ability to remember and to focus. As Dad's condition worsened, it became clear to everybody in the family that he must stop making financial decisions. So we all agreed that it was time to call a lawyer and order up a power of attorney.

When the paperwork was finished and the big day finally arrived, the whole family gathered in the lawyer's conference room. Floyd Leon was in a surprisingly good mood. As the attorney went through a big stack of papers and explained everything to my dad, everything went smoothly. But, as he was about to sign on the dotted line, my father's expression suddenly changed, his eyes misted over, and he put down the pen.

Something important had just occurred to Floyd Leon.

"I've just got one question," he said.

"Ask anything you'd like," replied the lawyer.

While Dad paused to gather his thoughts, the rest of us held our breath.

Then, my father asked a question that humbled everybody in that room.

"If I sign this paper," he asked, "can I still pay my tithe?"

When we assured Floyd Leon that he could still put his 10% in the offering plate every Sunday, Dad happily put his signature on the paper, and we all went home.

My father was willing to give up his silver—and give up total control over his finances—if, *and only if,* he could still give the Lord His fair share.

The rest of us should be just as concerned about giving God His portion of *our own* silver.

CHAPTER 14

SIGHT

Not long ago a crazy woman assaulted the Lego model of Mark Twain's house in the Hartford airport. A few crazy, lunging lurches and she threatened the entire Lego house. The folks in Jerusalem felt that way about the approaching army of Babylon. Their little city walls were as weak as a Lego model house. So the local citizens saw nothing but loss, envisioned nothing but despair, and thus expected nothing but destruction. Not Jeremiah. He saw what others could not see.

Indeed, the very Hebrew word for prophet means seer. Jeremiah saw decades ahead to the return of a purified people of God. He could see sturdy men building houses, laughing women going about their daily routines, and carefree children running through the little lanes of rebuilt Jerusalem. That's why we have no biblical books from the doom-seers but the longest of all prophecies from Jeremiah.

Jeremiah invested his silver because of his sight. His fearful neighbors saw only the invading Babylonian army descending on the tissue-thin defenseless walls of Jerusalem. But Jeremiah's sight was better.

The novelist David Courtland told of walking down the Washington, DC mall one day. He saw a group of folks coming toward him. When they got close enough, he saw that each of them had the distinctive white cane of the blind, everyone tapping along the street. The blind leader of the blind sensed Courtland's presence and made a surprising request: "Would you please take our picture?" That scrambled his brain. Why would a group of blind folks want their picture taken? It bothered him for the rest of the day.

By the evening he finally resolved the nagging question. Even though they were blind, those folks at the DC mall still believed in sight. That's the essence of those who plant shade trees for others to sit under.

We cannot see the future now. We are blind to it. The future hides behind the impenetrable wall of our own mortality, the curtain of time we cannot part, and the veil of mystery that always belongs to the future. Those who plant shade trees look behind all of that in faith and see what God can do *with eyes of faith.*

The author of Hebrews 11:1 lived in the same world as his great Hebrew ancestor Jeremiah: "Now faith is the substance of things hoped for and the evidence of things not seen." That is, the realm in which faith operates is the future ("things hoped for") and the invisible ("things not seen").

If you live only in the present and the visible, you do not live by faith. Faith looks at what cannot be seen in the future. Hebrews 11 gives a list of those who lived in that way. Abraham walked out into the desert going without knowing where, waiting on God without knowing when, and believing God without knowing how (Heb. 11:8-12).

In that regard, Jeremiah and Abraham were like United States sailors in World War II who sailed under sealed orders. There was something mysterious about the captain on the bridge of a battleship receiving a sealed envelope with degrees of latitude and longitude, those invisible lines that cross in the midst of the sea, written on the outside of the envelope.

The ship would throw off the mooring hawsers that held it to the dock, slip out into the harbor and into the icy Atlantic, and sail without knowing where. When the captain reached those coordinates, he would open the envelope. Sometimes it would contain another set of numbers, instructing the captain to head for some different location, again, without knowing "next where." Into the future the ship sailed, believing that a meaningful destination would be determined by those faithfully giving the commands.

In one sense, all of us who have faith are sailing under sealed orders in the life of faith. We go without knowing "next where," and we wait, without knowing when. God knows, and we trust that. God guides, and we believe that.

If you live in the world of the future and the invisible, you bank your life on the reality of God. You trust what you cannot yet see.

Paul states it plainly: "Fix your gaze on what you cannot see; if you can see it, it is not going to last. Only what you cannot see is going to last" (2 Cor. 4:18, Swan's Revised Version).

When I was in high school Mrs. Seale taught us about oxymorons. An oxymoron is a contradiction: high lowness, near farness, wet dryness, or Red-Neck intelligence. Well, old Paul uses an oxymoron in 2 Corinthians 2:18. He writes about looking at what you cannot see, gazing at what is invisible or, to be literal, assessing with acuity what is unseen. He uses the word that gives us "scope." A telescope sees things in space you cannot see, a microscope sees things so small you cannot see them, and a stethoscope hears things so quiet you cannot hear them. You get the idea.

Jeremiah looked out decades into a future that no one else could see. He saw beyond the desert death march that took the Jews over 600 miles as refugees into a foreign land. He saw beyond their trials in Babylon where Ezekiel would give them his mysterious visions. He saw beyond the sudden edict of Cyrus the Iranian who would suddenly surprise them by sending them back home. He saw beyond Nehemiah building a new wall for Jerusalem and Ezra helping to build the new Temple. He saw children laughing, vineyards growing, and life happening where there had been no life. Yet, while Jeremiah was seeing all of this, no one else saw anything except defeat and depression.

That is how faith always acts. It sees past what is right in front of it. You are in a marital mess? Faith sees beyond that and looks at happiness. You are ill? Faith sees the time you will be whole again, either here or on the other side. You are broke? Faith sees God's provision coming from strange places that you simply cannot imagine. But that's not all.

People with substance, those folks who have been blessed with material wealth, need to have *particularly* good vision. They need to see that Bible translator on a tiny island in the middle of the Pacific Ocean. They need to see that missionary in a rain forest in Brazil handing native people Bibles that they cannot even read. People with more stuff than they can use may look at a trashy vacant lot in Haiti and see an orphanage that isn't yet built, filled with children who are not yet born.

People who can afford to forego a luxury may endow a missionary they will never meet, who takes the Word of God to people they will never see, in a language they will never hear. That's the oxymoron of seeing what is invisible.

Jeremiah had only one friend during his life, Baruch. Jeremiah's own family tried to take him out, the king despised him, and his generation misunderstood him. Nobody remembers any of them. But in millions of homes, millions of Bibles have Jeremiah's book because he saw the invisible.

CHAPTER 15

SIGNATURE

What is the most expensive autograph in the world? Most experts say it's the signature of William Shakespeare. Only six known signatures of Shakespeare have been discovered. Appraisers estimate that any one of those signatures would bring $4 million. The highest price ever paid for an autograph on the open market was $748,000 for an 1863 signature of Abraham Lincoln on a document defending the Emancipation Proclamation. The oldest known autograph may be from 2600 B.C. in cuneiform writing by a scribed name Abu. That would make it 4,600 years old.

Yet for the purposes of God, none of those signatures had the significance of an autograph that was penned about 2,600 years ago: the signature of Jeremiah on the deed for the field he bought from his kinsman Hanamel (Jer. 32:10).

In the presence of witnesses Jeremiah signed the deed indicating his purchase of a field that would belong to the enemy. When he signed the deed, other witnesses signed the deed in front of the ancient equivalent of a notary (32:12). Jeremiah did not express a vague wish, a whimsical hope, or a cheap desire. He put his name on the line. With his name, he pledged himself to buy the property and left a public record of what he had done. The deed was placed for safekeeping in a clay jar, the safety deposit box of its day.

A whole tribe of wannabe's, might-have-been's, could-have-been's, and the ones that got away litter the landscape of human life. Franz Schubert started his "Unfinished Symphony" in 1822. He completed only two movements even though he lived another six years. To this day musicologists argue about why he did not finish the thing. It stands as a monument to that which was never completed. Notes were never played by an orchestra that never sat before an audience that never gathered, all because it was unfinished. Jeremiah did not leave an unfinished symphony of intent. He believed in Nike theology: he just did it.

Only April 12, 1945, Elizabeth Shoumatoff was painting President Franklin D. Roosevelt at his Little White House near Warm Springs, Georgia. At midday they took a break for lunch. During lunch FDR complained of a terrible pain in the back of his head. At 3:35 p.m. he was pronounced dead.

You can see the unfinished portrait of FDR hanging in a special place in the Little White House of Warm Springs. Only his face is finished and the rest of the painting is only roughed in. Roosevelt sat for the portrait but died before it could be done. Jeremiah did not leave a half-finished portrait of his intention. You have the full picture. He moved beyond mere wish and hope to completion and execution. He placed his signature on the deed.

Every salesperson knows the significance of getting that signature. My friend the late, great motivational speaker Zig Zigler once told of the story of a last-sales-pitch-of-the-day he made while he was trying to sell kitchenware. At the time, Zig was broke, his wife was expecting a baby, and he was pitching some not-so-well-known brand of kitchenware. At the end of his pitch he simply looked at the lady client. Exasperated with his reluctance, she finally told him, "Young man, you have to ask for the order."

The critical moment in any sales pitch is when the salesman turns the contract around on the table so that it is right-side-up to the client and upside down to the salesman. He sticks out a pen towards the client and holds it in the air. He asks for the signature. As Zig's brother once said, "Timid salesmen have skinny kids." The signature is the moment of truth, the defining act. So it was for Jeremiah. Buying the field at Anathoth was a theory, a wish, a dream, and a fiction until he signed that deed. We should never deceive ourselves that stopping short of the signature actually concludes the matter.

Life's most important documents are nothing without that signature. You may have a $100,000 wedding, but absent the minister's signature on the marriage license it did not happen. You may have earned a PhD, but absent the university president's signature on the diploma, you have nothing. You may have a million-dollar check, but absent a signature, you have a lot of zeroes and nothing else.

The 56 signers of the Declaration of Independence abide as the true founders of the United States. Pamphlets, editorials, books, debates, and speeches abounded before the America Revolution but did not change the situation. It was only when 56 men placed their names on a document declaring the United States to be independent of Great Britain that the world moved on its hinges. It took their signatures; it took an executed document.

Even the apostle Paul authenticated the genuineness of his most intense and confronting epistle, Galatians, with large letters in his own hand (Gal. 6:11). He attested his genuine authorship of a New Testament epistle with his signature towards the end. But one of the most famous signatures in the Bible was the signature of Jeremiah on the deed to the field at Anatoth (Jer. 32:10). In the presence of witnesses he put his name on the line when he made a purchase that, to the entire world, looked crazy. He bought the field under the army of his nation's enemies. Up to that time he was only in a coulda, woulda, shoulda situation. All hat and no cattle. But, when he put his signature on the line, it changed everything.

Even in a digital world, signatures are still required. You cannot buy a house, get a hunting license, execute a legal document, get married, or get buried without a signature. No one would consider a high school or college diploma valid without the executive's signature plus others for good measure. Major events in this life require that certain documents be executed. To get things done, you've still got to sign on the dotted line.

Can you imagine what Jeremiah might have done short of putting his John Hancock on the document? He could have insisted on going back for one more inspection of the property ("Can't be sure without taking another look"). Or he might have insisted that he see the property on a sunny day when there was no wind ("Can't make a big decision in bad weather"). Or he might have insisted that just the right witnesses be present to observe the signing of the deed ("Can't let just anybody be a witness"). Or he might have insisted on a different kind of clay jar to put the deed into once it had been signed ("Can't be too careful about the quality of your safety-deposit jar"). And so forth, and so forth, on and on, without doing a blessed thing.

A hillbilly needed an ax. Only one man on the hill had an ax. He went to the man with the ax and said, "Neighbor, I need to borrow your ax."

"I'm eatin' black-eyed peas," his hillbilly neighbor replied.

"You didn't hear me. All I need is to just borrow your ax."

"I done told ya once. I'm eatin' peas."

This curious conversation went on with the same question and the same answer for 10 minutes. They were kind of slow. Finally, the man needing the ax asked, "What the heck do eatin' peas have to do with loanin' your ax?"

The response settled the question: "When you don't want to loan yer ax, one excuse is as good as the other."

When you do not want to execute, or do the thing, or finally cross the line and say that you're all in, any excuse at all will do.

I heard the story of a sales manager for a door-to-door sales firm. When one of the salesmen failed to show up for the Monday-morning sales meeting, the sales manager wanted an answer. The would-be-salesman responded, "I was cleaning the grass out of my lawnmower blades." When you want to find an excuse, you can even blame it on the grass!

Nowhere is excuse-making more significant than in the decisions we make for God. I belong to the Baptist tribe. We have a custom that is strange to some folk, but it belongs to the very fabric of who we are. We ask folks at the end of the sermon if they want to stand up, get out of their seats, and walk down the aisle to indicate a spiritual decision. And yes, we give them a card to sign on the spot. That may seem quaint, but we want them to sign on the dotted line right there. It is our way of showing folks that "you're either in or out." Then, after they've signed up, we dunk them under water and hold them there until they say "tithe."

Your church may do it with a confirmation class, or the bishop may put his hands on your head or some other ceremony. Every church I know of has some ceremony which says that "now, you're all in." When Jeremiah fixed his name to those ancient scrolls, he left a testimony about where he stood and what his commitments were.

Millions of people have waited in line at the National Archives Building in Washington, DC to look at the fading signatures of the original signers of the Declaration of Independence. That document is the charter of our nation and a testimony to men who risked their lives to get the whole thing started.

The Declaration of Independence is physical evidence of where those men stood. The same was true with Jeremiah. As those old clay jars held the deeds through the generations, a father would bring a son and that son would bring his son and point to the jars as the containers of the future of Israel. The deeds and the jars kept hope alive, kept the promise alive, made the future real to all who saw them.

When we sign something, others take hope from what we signed.

On March 6, 1836, Col. William Barrett Travis had known for several days that his situation inside the old Spanish mission called the Alamo had become hopeless. Several thousand soldiers under the command of Mexican Gen. Antonio Lopez de Santa Anna had Travis and some 189 other defenders surrounded.

The young Texas colonel, only 26 years old, was not a professional military man. But Travis knew enough history to understand that in a siege, the army on the outside usually prevails over the army on the inside. So he gathered his fellow defenders that Saturday afternoon and gave them a speech.

"We must die," he began. "Our business is not to make a fruitless effort to save our lives, but to choose the manner of our death."

He saw three possibilities: Surrender and summary execution, trying to fight their way out only to be "butchered" by Mexican lancers, or "remain in this fort, resist every assault, and to sell our lives as dearly as possible."

Then, with a flourish, Travis drew his sword and slowly marked a line in the dirt. "I now want every man who is determined to stay here and die with me to come across this line."

Young Tapley Holland made his decision quickly, proclaiming, "I am ready to die for my country!" as he jumped over the line. It's hard to picture it as a stampede—the men knew they were voting to die—yet all but two of them walked over the line. Co-commander Jim Bowie, lying sick on a cot, asked some of his men to carry him across. Only Louis Moses Rose, a French soldier of fortune, remained behind. That night, Rose slipped out of the Alamo and managed to make it through the enemy lines. He ended up in Louisiana and supposedly lived until 1850.

Every Texan knows what happened the morning after Rose made his escape. In the predawn of March 6, Santa

Anna's forces breached the walls and killed every Texas combatant.

This event gave to the world the phrase, "a line in the sand." It is one of the great metaphors of history. To "cross the line in the sand" means to do the deed, make the commitment, make obvious what you intend to do.

For those men at the Alamo, stepping across that line meant death. But when it comes to the kingdom of God, stepping across the line means crossing from certain death into eternal life. When we put who we are and what we have across the line in the work of God's kingdom, we are crossing a line from bondage to freedom, from greed to grace, from having to giving.

Isn't it time for you to cross the line, to put your signature on a deed to the future? That is how you plant shade trees that others sit under. Write your name, make your mark, put down an "X" that marks the spot where you'll begin planting. That way, you'll be assured that the tress you plant will be the ones God has led you to plant!

If you divided up the 5.2 million trees in New York City among the population of that huge place, the total would come out to 5/8 of a tree for every resident of the city. Now that is a curious thought for the Ole Swan. Who wants 5/8 of a tree? Give me a whole tree or a small forest, but I am not interested in 5/8 of a tree. What happened to the other 3/8?

My high school business law teacher, Mrs. Sue Ellen

Foster, always wanted us to find where the rest of the fraction was. I doubt that she ever thought about 3/8 of a tree. If you are going to plant a tree, you need to plant the whole tree, not a fraction of tree.

In reality, what that statistic means is that a whole bunch of folks in New York City have never planted a tree. Some folks planted multiple trees, and some planted none. That means a lot of folks are sitting under the shade of trees someone else planted. Go figure. You either sit under someone else's shade tree or plant one for somebody else.

In the words of the Holy Bible, there comes a time to perform the doing of it (2 Cor. 8:11). We can preach, pray, meet, exhort, encourage, demonstrate, model, and promote, but at the end of all of that, there comes a time to perform the doing of it, to use Paul's words. And when you plant a shade tree, you really cannot plant 5/8 of a tree.

A moment comes in many endeavors when a decision must be made.

The speed at which an airplane takes off is called V2. This is the speed at which the plane can safely become airborne. Yet before that plane reaches V2, there's a decision-point called V1. You see, when the plane reaches the speed V1, that pilot is committed to take off. V1 is at a point of no return. You cannot change your mind and go back to the gate. After you reach V1, you have to go.

For a small plane, V1 might be 60 mph, but for a big

Boeing 747, it could be 170 mph, give or take. When you have reached those speeds, you are beyond the point of no return. You are committed to take off. There is an invisible line on every runway. It is a mathematical line. It is not painted on the runway. It should be in the pilot's mind: beyond this line, the pilot must take off. It's the "go or no-go" line. And it's a very important line to understand.

When it comes to planting shade trees, there should be an invisible line in your mind. You have thought about it, moved toward it, are right next to it. Now, it's time for take-off. You know it is time for you to plant a shade tree, to make a commitment, and to do the thing that God has put on your heart. It may be at your church; it could be for your kid's future; it might be for a missionary enterprise, or for an investment in a Christian non-profit ministry. You are at V1, and you need to take off. But, please don't wait for "perfect" conditions to lift off because conditions are never absolutely perfect.

If you're waiting for the perfect moment to act, you'll be waiting for a long time. Life never presents you with picture-perfect conditions. One of the arresting stories in world history was the decision to launch D-Day, the largest invasion in history and the military moment that saved the free world.

The weather on June 5, 1944, was terrible. Many suggested to Supreme Allied Commander Dwight D. Eisenhower that the landing be postponed for two weeks, a disastrous delay in light of the situation. In the middle of the night, an unknown Scot, Group Captain Stagg, promised Eisenhower there would be a break in the weather on June 6, 1944. Others said there would not be. Ike had to make the decision.

The moment came at 4:15 a.m. on June 5, 1944, when Ike famously said, "OK, let's go." Those words launched the largest armada in history and started the end of World War II. Ike had his V1 moment, and he responded. When he did, 5,000 ships and a multitude of soldiers moved together, toward the victory that would ultimately come.

Your life is like that. You look at what you have. You look at the work God has placed on your heart. You look in the faces of those whose lives will be changed forever by your willingness to plant a shade tree, and you come to the moment to say, "OK, let's go."

Ike's go-or-no-go decision was made in the dark, under conditions that were far from perfect. Very few shade trees are planted in perfect conditions. Booth did not begin the Salvation Army under perfect conditions. My alma mater Baylor did not start in 1845 under perfect conditions. For that matter, the capital of the United States was not built under perfect conditions. The Potomac basin was a hot, humid, muddy, swampy, mosquito-infested backwater that was transformed into a beautiful city in the hardest of times.

There is never a perfect time to begin a job, to organize a company, to start a degree, to initiate an exercise program, to get married, or to start a family. As one girl said, "I spent my life looking for Mr. Right and found out that life only brings you Mr. Almost-Right." (Lauree, you do not have to comment on that, please.) Life consists of making decisions—and acting upon them—despite imperfect circumstances and an uncertain future. Whatever it is that you're about to do, you can be sure of this: there's never a "perfect" time to get started.

The first report usually seems loaded with negatives: the task is too hard, the enemies are too big, and the time is not right. After seeing the mighty acts of the God who delivered them from Egypt, the Hebrews came to the border of the Promised Land. Rather than go forward into the future God had for them, they sent out a committee of 12 spies, 10 of whom came back with reports of giants in the land. They quivered with fear as they cried that the Hebrews looked like grasshoppers to those giants (Num. 13:33).

Only two valiant men, Joshua and Caleb, dared to believe they could stare down the giants and move into the Promised Land. The names of the fearful ten are forgotten forever, but thousands of boys this year will be named Joshua and Caleb in memory of those two who seized the moment.

I have forgotten most of what I ever knew of the Latin language (and I didn't know very much to begin with). But I do remember one Latin phrase that is still used in the English language. That phrase is *Carpe diem*. Those two words say it best and in short order: Seize the day.

The people who plant shade trees are those who seize the day, grab the moment, and cross the line. They do not procrastinate, waffle, hedge, dodge, pass the buck, whine, or hide behind a skinny excuse. First, they decide, and then *they act.*

Right now I wish I could sit down at your kitchen table over a cup of coffee or a cola and look you right in the eye, just Ole Swan and you. If I could—and I would if I could—I would ask you if you have the sensitivity of a Jeremiah, a man who felt deeply the need of the moment. I would ask you to open your eyes. Down the street, across the country, or around the world, there is an "X" that marks the spot where God wants you to plant a shade tree.

From the moment God created this planet, your "X" has been there. When God called order out of chaos, day out of night, being out of nothingness, God put that "X" out there in the future for you to plant a shade tree. God put that "X" in the field of Anatoth for Jeremiah. He put an "X" in Chicago for Moody to start a Bible institute. He put an "X" on the Upper West Side of New York City for John D. Rockefeller Sr. to build a towering church. If you are sensitive, you will find it; there is an "X" marked for you somewhere. The problem is not the absence of the "X," but the presence of sensitivity.

CHAPTER 16

SHADE TREES PLANTED FOR ME

While I was at Baylor University, I was so honored to serve as a minister of youth at Columbus Avenue Baptist Church. There were so many shade-tree planters there for me. I've already mentioned Dr. Marshall Edwards, but there were others, like Dr. Ron Durham who was the associate pastor and my direct supervisor—he was like a Barnabas to me. I'll love him forever.

The laypeople at Columbus Avenue were like family to me as I majored in Greek and religion at Baylor from 1972-1976. Charlie and Gertrude Marstaller were my adopted parents. I lived with them in the summers—they fed me, advised me, confronted me, and loved me. They "signed up" to mentor me and parent me in so many ways. With their words they made their "mark" to "adopt" me that first summer following my fall and spring semesters. They said, "We will take him," and they did. Wow! I love the Marstallers!

There are dozens of other stories, but I must tell this one about a great gentleman whom I didn't know very well but he helped me in a great time of need. When I was leaving Baylor to attend Southwestern Baptist Theological Seminary (now that is a mouthful) in the fall of 1976, all I had were my clothes, books, and an old Fiat. I had paid for my first month's rent at an apartment that I would share with three other seminary buddies, and I had about $200 in cash . . . pastorally speaking—probably closer to $100.

My last week on the job with Columbus Avenue, my car died. (It had a transmission coronary.) I was devastated. But the word got out, and Dr. Edwards, "Rabbi," shared my situation with Oliver "Rev" Winchell, the owner of Central Texas Ironworks.

People knew Mr. Winchell as "Rev" because when he was a boy he and his buddies played a game where they would spell each other's names backward. His real name was Oliver, which was a mouthful to say and even a bigger mouthful to spell backwards, "Revilo". So, to make things easier, they shortened it to Rev.

A lot of folks in the church probably thought he was a retired preacher—many folks didn't know that he was one of the wealthiest men in the church. Rev and Marshall were very close, so close that one day Mr. Winchell showed up at Marshall's office with his lawyer. They had a document that stated Mr. Winchell would do anything that his pastor asked him to do! And, he signed that document in front of his attorney and Dr. Edwards. No doubt, he loved and trusted his pastor.

Mr. Winchell was close to 80, and we didn't really know each other that well, but I'll never forget his phone call. I answered the phone, and he said, "Dennis, I hear you've got your tail in a crack."

Well, I hope I haven't offended you . . . but that's what he said . . . I'm just giving my testimony!

The call sort of startled me. I thought to myself, well I'm really OK—I just need to find another car to take me 105 miles north to seminary in Ft. Worth.

I said, "Oh, no sir, I'm OK!"

He said, "No, you're not. I heard that your car broke down. I've prayed about it, and I want to buy you a new car."

I couldn't believe my ears. I replied, "Mr. Winchell, I don't know what to say."

He said, "Don't say anything. Just go find a good one and bring me the price. I'll write you a check. Then you go pick it up and head on to the seminary."

I called my dad and told him about it. My father, the famous Floyd Leon, who grew up as a sharecropper and was a printer for 45 years before he retired, said, "Son, you tell that man no! He needs to give that gift to some people who really need it!"

I said, "Dad, we *are* those people!" to which he replied,

"What a man . . . what a man . . . what a generous Christian."

I found a 1976 Ford Pinto—basic and plain—but it got me around. Of course, I later found out that it was a defective model. If you ever got hit in the rear, you and your Pinto could get blown up! But the Lord was my protector.

Anyway when I picked out the Pinto, I told Mr. Winchell the cost. Then I drove over to his house and picked up the check. I took the check to the dealership, and they couldn't believe Mr. Winchell's generosity. I couldn't believe it either (I was living a Billy Graham movie).

I picked up that Pinto and started driving it to his house. Man, it had the "new car smell" and everything. I had it loaded with all my belongings when I pulled into his driveway, got out, and rang the doorbell.

Mr. Winchell opened the door, looked at the Pinto, and asked, "Does your tail feel any better?"

I said, "Yes sir, Mr. Winchell. Yes sir!" I thanked him, hugged him, and then drove off. I was officially on my way to seminary.

At the last intersection before I got onto I-35 in Waco to head up to Ft. Worth, I was crying like a baby. Through my tears, I looked at the car next to me. Beside me in her car was a lady and her two small kids. When she saw my tears, she began crying too! Perhaps she saw my Pinto filled to the brim with all my worldly possessions. She probably thought I had just said goodbye to my loved ones. Little did she know I was driving a *huge* shade tree given to me by "Rev" Winchell, my forever brother in Christ.

Mr. Winchell didn't live long after that, but his "shade" —his influence, his generosity, and his love—remain with me to this day.

I remember talking to "Rabbi" about it later. I asked, "How can I ever pay Mr. Winchell back?"

He said, "Dennis, you can't pay him back, but one day you can do the same for someone else!"

Praise the Lord, Lauree and I have been able to do just that. What a joy it was for us to sign our name next to the "X" that MARKED the spot to provide a vehicle for two twin boys going to college. I can still see their smiles as they jumped in the front seat of that mustang. Thank you, "Rev," for teaching me "The Joy of the Shade Tree."

CHAPTER 17

X MARKS THE SPOT: *YOUR X, YOUR SPOT*

God will show you your "X." Ask Him and He will show you the "X" that marks your particular spot, the one He has specially picked up for you. God leads, guides, and speaks, especially when you ask Him to show you where you need to plant a shade tree.

Seeing the "X" that marks the spot requires a moment of surrender. To see something is to know it rationally. But rationality then needs to sink deep into your emotions so that you feel in your heart what you know in your head. Even ole Aristotle said that folks don't surrender without deeply feeling what they know.

There is a Bible translator who will give her life to bury herself alive with a tribe in the rainforest, to live with them, to study their language, to learn their culture, and then to give them a Bible in a language that never had the word of God. Feel that!

She has a family she will leave; she turns her back on a career that would pay her 10 times as much; she refuses a home in an affluent neighborhood with kinfolk nearby. Why? To go plant herself alive as a shade tree in the very place God wants her to be. She has surrendered.

Will you surrender to help her make that sacrifice? Missions and evangelism deserve our resources so that we can plant shade trees that will enable "those who will go" to carry out the Great Commission while obeying the Great Commandment.

When you sense it and surrender to it, there comes a moment for you to reach for your silver. Jeremiah did just that and he did so under circumstances less ideal than you will, gentle reader.

Jeremiah was a marked man, a prisoner, a reject, an untouchable. He was a depressed and disappointed servant of God. Yet he seized the moment to plant his "X" forever in a field at Anatoth. And he could not do so without his silver, the substance of his life.

The best way to look at money is liquid life, concentrated living, printed personal energy, engraved influence on a piece of paper owned by Uncle Sam. You work, you earn, you invest, you gain—all under the blessing of God. Although those bills have Hamilton and Lincoln and Franklin printed on them, they could just as well have your face printed on them. They are a concentrated evidence of your gifts, your talents, your thrift, your willingness to risk, your education, your influence, and your energy.

Money is printed, concentrated life. When you take it out of your bank account and plant a shade tree with it, you have used your energy and your life to do something at the "X" that God has marked for you.

Planting shade trees that you'll never sit under requires vision, insight, and foresight. Jeremiah had 20/20 spiritual vision as he surmised the situation. The Babylonians were taking over the Holy City Jerusalem, and the process of deporting God's people to Babylon was already underway. It was the worst of times—everybody figured it was all over for the holy city.

Nevertheless, Jeremiah, with his Father's eyes could "see the invisible." He could even see 70 years into the future. He could see houses and fields and shade trees, if you will, in Jerusalem one fine day. God revealed these things to the prophet who would not personally profit from his act of faith. Jeremiah didn't reap personal rewards, but others did.

So he bought the field at Anathoth because he could see God's people returning one day to Jerusalem. And sure enough, 70 years later, the Persians defeated the Babylonians and Cyrus eventually told God's people they could go home. When they did, they had a place to live—Anathoth—all because Jeremiah was sensitive because he surrendered, because he gave his silver, and because he had faith. When the time for signing arrived, Jeremiah did exactly that. He planted a shade tree for others, not for himself.

God sees you. He speaks to you. He evokes from your heart surrender; He gives you sight, and He gives you the opportunity to "sign on" and "make your mark." God gives you an opportunity to become a shade-tree planter.

Jeremiah made his mark. He signed those documents and placed them in an earthen jar in front because the papers he signed needed to last a longtime, which turned out to be 70 years. But those seeds sprouted, and God's people were blessed because Jeremiah planted shade trees that he never sat under.

How can we do less when we recognize that God Himself is the Great Shade-Tree Planter. He planted a beautiful garden in Eden and told the first humans they could have every tree except one. How generous He was. The Bible that begins with a garden ends in the Revelation with *another* garden filled with trees for the healing of the nations.

> When you plant a shade tree, you are indeed imitating God, the greatest Planter of them all.

A garden of trees at the beginning and a garden of trees at the end! Those gardens are both there because of the garden in the middle, the Garden of Gethsemane, where Jesus prayed under those thousand-year-old olive trees.

Nathaniel was meditating under a tree when Jesus saw him and called him. Zaccheus climbed up a tree to see Jesus. Taller and stronger and higher is the greatest tree of all, the Cross where Jesus died, a tree called Calvary. When you plant a shade tree you are indeed imitating God, the greatest Planter of them all.

CHAPTER 18

WHEN A HANDSHAKE IS AS GOOD AS A SIGNATURE

He made his mark, his signature, by giving me his handshake.

I was at my last pastorate in the early '90s in West Monroe, Louisiana when I had followed a pastor who had served the church for 29 years. My predecessor was a faithful man and a wonderful, beloved pastor. I was young and energetic—and an initiator of change!

Whoa—did I say "change"? "Change" is not a safe word in a Baptist church! That's probably why, looking back, I was only there four years. Some would call me the "transition" pastor or the "change-agent" servant leader. Well, I guess you could say I "knocked over a few hurdles for the next guy."

Nevertheless, we had experienced growth and excitement. The church had plateaued at about 1,000 folks for that past three decades, and now we were running about 1,200 and baptizing 100 people a year.

There was a sense of a "new day" in the history of our church, and we needed a children's building to serve an expanding number of young people. The children's facility would be a "shade tree" that would allow the church to become what it is today: a church that has exploded from 1,000 in average attendance to almost 3,000.

I'll always remember going to see Sidney Wilhite—my friend—the kind of guy who is a "preacher's buddy."

Sidney is what he is: he shoots straight; he tells it like it is, and his bark ain't as bad as his bite . . . most of the time.

Good thing about Sidney is that he lets you let your hair down, too. He lets you be a *man* as well as a preacher man. He's one of my all-time favorites.

Entering Sidney's office, I once again noticed the unassuming décor, some stuffed game on the walls—some guns, a few of which were Civil War antiques—and there was Sid, in a tan khaki shirt and khaki pants. But don't let the looks fool ya. Sidney started a plastic recycling company in the early '70s (remember the movie *The Graduate*, and the famous line about investing: "Plastics, son, plastics.")

Well, Sidney and his sons, John Mark and Ross, have done quite well—they ship plastics all over the country, and maybe all over the world. Sidney's success was "big time" way before my TV show *Swan's Place* was "sweet" and *Duck*

Dynasty was "cool" in West Monroe, Louisiana.

I had brought a painting of the proposed children's building with me, and I was even more nervous about that because that painting cost me a bundle. But the experts told me that a picture is worth a thousand words.

I had the picture sort of hid behind me, but Sidney noticed it when I came through the door. You don't pull anything on Sidney. Anyway, we exchanged some good-ol-boy talk, but shortly he cut to the chase: "OK, Swan, what ya want? You need some money?"

> Plant something now in your own sphere of influence. Ask God where to plant it.

I said, "Now, Sidney, I want to show you a picture," and I placed the artist's rendering of the children's building in his lap.

"Well," he said, "this is nice. So what do you want from me?"

My throat was a bit dry, but with every bit of energy I could muster, standing straight and tall—acting like I had marching orders from Jesus Himself—I said, "I need a MIL-LION DOLLARS to get this building program off dead center . . . and I want you to do it for YOUR MOMMA!"

"Did I hear you right?" he asked. "A million dollars? Even the university doesn't ask me for that kind of money."

"I know it," I said. "But I'm not the university, And, I'm asking you to do it for your momma!"

Sidney said, "You're getting pretty heavy now, preacher!!"

Then, there was a long pause. Sidney leaned back in his chair, and my heart continued to race. My vision of the children's building was a bit blurry, and I was trying to ready myself for rejection.

And as best I remember, I spoke next. I said, "Sidney, I want you to do it for the Lord and for your mom."

Sidney's mother, Floy Antley Wilhite, had worked in our children's department for 30 years. She had confided to several of her closest friends that she had prayed often that Sidney would do something very special for the kingdom of God someday. Well, this special lady had passed away—yet in her prayer life, she had planted a shade tree that she would never sit under but others would.

After Sidney had paused for a few moments to let my words sink in, he stood up and shook my hand. Then he asked, "How do you want it?"

I said, "Could you give one-third of it every year for three years?"

He looked me straight into my eyes and said, "OK, I'll do it!"

I think I hugged him. And Sidney, by the way, ain't big on huggin'.

Then I left, climbed into my car, and drove back to the

church. When I arrived, I looked at the lot, and I saw it. I saw a three-story building that would hold 400 precious souls for the glory of God. Many other precious saints would also sacrifice to make that building a reality, but Sidney and his family planted an awfully big shade tree that day.

Sidney made his mark that day; he gave his signature, with a handshake.

Sometime later, after the building was built, he told me that out of all the benevolent things he had done, this was the greatest. By the way, a few years later, Sidney and his family planted an additional shade tree by adding on to the children's building with a pre-school building.

Sidney is a true shade-tree planter. Matter of fact, Sidney and his wife, Charline, take great delight today in planting actual shade trees at their home and farm for their kids and grandkids.

When the moment presented itself to him to plant, Sidney didn't delay. He acted; he just did it. I pray that as God reveals to you the shade tree He wants you to plant, you will do it! I pray that you'll sign on the dotted line. I pray that you will place your name next to the "mark" or to the "X" on the pledge/commitment card. Or, if it's your style, I pray that you'll give a heavenly Handshake.

Plant something now in your own sphere of influence. Ask God where to plant it. A church, a family, a school, a non-profit, a ministry, or the mission field. Seize this day, grasp this moment, and maximize this hour.

On that great day, when the Lord of the servants returns and asks us what we did with the resources He left in our hands, may we be sure we can point to a shade tree we planted. Remember that "X" marks the spot.

The kingdom of God awaits your participation.

CHAPTER 19

THE REST OF *TWO* STORIES: A GREAT-GRANDDAD AND A *GREAT* GRANDDAD

I've already introduced you to two amazing men: my great-grandfather Aron Johnson (whom I never met) and my dear granddad Elof Swanberg (whom I always adored, and still do). Now, I'd like to tell you the rest of *their* stories.

WHO WILL TAKE HIS PLACE?

Years ago, we discovered that Aron Johnson was not only a farmer but also a part-time preacher. In fact, Aron was ordained by the Methodist Episcopal Church in 1898. That meant that whenever the full-time pastor was away, Aron could fill in and preach Sunday services from the pulpit. And that's exactly what he did.

I'll always believe that Aron intended to make the ministry his profession. But we'll never know for sure because, while he was still a full-time farmer—even before his last child was born—Aron took sick and died.

After the funeral, Aron's pastor penned a letter that now hangs on my legacy wall, in the hallway of our home. In describing my great-grandfather, the pastor wrote, "He was like the giant oak that fell in the midst of the storm. Who will take his place?" When I read that line for the first time, I instantly said, "I will. I will take his place."

That was over 20 years ago, and I'm still taking Aron Johnson's place today. That's why I'm not slowing down. That's why I'm still traveling and preaching 170 days each year. I refuse to slow down because I know that my great-grandfather planted a shade tree for me that he never sat under: Aron instilled the love of God in my family, but he didn't live long enough to achieve his dream of preaching the gospel full time. So I've taken his place.

Now, Aron and I are, in a very real sense, planting shade trees together.

A COTTON GIN, A LETTER, AND *Two* SHADE TREES

My granddad Elof Swanberg, the same fellow who came to America on the *Lusitania*, was essentially an indentured servant from the ages of 14 to 24. It took Elof 10 long years to pay back the cost of the one-way tickets that brought his sister and himself to America. Then, at age 24, when he was finally free of that debt, Elof became a sharecropper, which meant that most of the profits from his farming went to the landlord. But, Elof worked hard and saved what little he could.

In his forties, my granddad finally became a land owner when a Depression-era program allowed him to buy 100 acres from Uncle Sam. According to the paperwork, Elof had 40 years to pay back the government, but he didn't intend to wait that long. So he planted crops on every inch of tillable land and worked in the fields from dawn to dusk.

One day, while leaning down over a big piece of farm equipment, my grandfather made a mistake that almost cost him his life. You see, Elof pushed his hand down just a little too far into a big piece of machinery called a cotton gin, and his hand became caught in the blades.

As my granddad's arm was pulled farther and farther into the machine, he screamed for his friend, Lee Anderson, who was also working in the field. Lee ran over and cut off the cotton gin, but my grandfather was still caught. It was obvious that Elof might bleed to death unless his friend could find some way to reverse the gears on the huge machine.

Using superhuman strength—strength that must have

come from God—Lee Anderson managed to grab the huge belt that powered the cotton gin and pull that belt backwards, reversing the blades, until Elof could pull his mangled arm free. Under normal circumstances, pulling that huge belt backwards was a job that might have required four or five strong men, but on that terrible day, Lee did it by himself.

Lee Anderson drove Elof to the hospital where they took off what remained of my grandpa's arm. It was a horrific experience, but it could have been much worse. Lee had saved my grandfather's life and, by doing so, had planted a massive shade tree for the entire Swanberg family.

Fast forward half a century. In 1995, I left my pastorate to begin a career as a full-time speaker. A year later, I was still making it, but a few doubts were starting to creep in. I began to wonder: "Is this *really* doing anybody any good?" Then, one day, I received a letter from a woman named Cynthia Sundbeck.

Cynthia said that she had been given one of my cassette tapes by a friend, and that the tape made a big difference in her life. She described the pain she had been feeling: a mixture of perfectionism and worry. Then, Cynthia told me that my message had made her laugh *and* think. She said the tape was a blessing because it encouraged her to take herself *and* her problems a little less seriously.

Cynthia also wrote that, as she listened to the tape, it occurred to her that the name Swanberg sounded familiar. So, she called her mother to inquire about me.

"Of course we know the Swanbergs," replied Cynthia's mother. "We've know them for years. In fact, we've known Dennis since he was knee-high to a grasshopper!"

Then, the mother added another piece of information that, for me, was a clear message from God. She said, "Cynthia, your grandfather, Lee Anderson, once pulled Dennis's granddad out of a cotton gin."

I was astounded.

I still have Cynthia Sundbeck's letter hanging on my "Legacy Wall". That letter is a reminder that Lee Anderson once planted a shade tree for my family and that, many years later, God gave me the opportunity to plant a shade tree for Lee's grand-daughter.

I guess you could say that when it comes to shade-tree planting, what goes around comes around!

THERE'S STILL TIME

Elof Swanberg planted his own shade trees. Aron Johnson planted shade trees, too. So did Lee Anderson, Miss Mary Leila Ellington, Marshall Edwards, Oliver "Rev" Winchell, Sidney Wilhite, and all the other planters I've mentioned in this book.

Now, it's your turn.

You still have enough time to plant each and every shade tree that God is calling you to plant. He's speaking to your heart, and He wants you to decide for Him. But you don't have an eternity to make up your mind. So, as you think about your own life and about the things you'd like to accomplish while you still have time, please remember the five key traits of a shade-tree planter:

SENSITIVITY
You must be sensitive to God's voice;

SURRENDER
You must surrender to God's calling;

SILVER
You must be willing to invest your time,
your talents, and your money;

SIGHT
You must have a vision of the future,
a mental image of God's plan for your unique gift
or your particular contribution;

SIGNATURE
When the time for action comes, you must be willing to sign
your name and seal your pledge.

Today, like every other day, is planting season.

God has prepared the ground for you. Now, it's time for action. The needs are great, and the workers are few. That's why the trees you're about to plant are so important.

May God bless you as you plant those shade trees. Your planting will be eternal, and ultimately you will receive your shade-tree reward in heaven, for that is where your heart *now* and forever *will be.*

*But STORE UP for Yourselves
Treasures in heaven, where neither
moth nor rust destroys, and
where thieves do not break in or steal,
for where your treasure is,
there your heart will be also.*

—

Matthew 6:20-21

STUDY SESSIONS

BY JOHN POWERS AND DENNIS SWANBERG

APPLYING THE INSIGHTS OF
PLANTING SHADE TREES

SHADE TREE SESSION ONE

PLANTING SHADE TREES
"Lessons from a Walk in the Woods"

The Swan's discovery of the magnificence and beauty of Muir Woods (pp. 19–21) helps us grasp the importance of shade trees. It's possible to become a shade tree too! How? According to Psalm 1:3, "He will be like a tree firmly planted by streams of water, which yields its fruit in its season and it's leaf does not wither; and in whatever he does, he prospers" (NASB).

In light of Psalm 1:3, what promise(s) does the Bible offer to anyone who applies God's Word?

_____

_____

_____

_____

Yes we, too, can become shade trees! As a matter of fact, an important first key to planting shade trees is becoming a shade tree! What pathway might one use to becoming a shade tree? Some might Google "trees" and merely dream about visiting a forest of giant redwoods. Others could read

Joyce Kilmer's classic poem, "Trees," and long to revisit care-free childhood years. But dreaming and reflecting about trees doesn't aid in the process of becoming a shade tree. It takes action and passion. It takes heart! At some point in life, we must value becoming a shade tree. Like the redwoods of Muir Woods need one another, someone, somewhere, sometime will need you. Believers are not islands to themselves. Has God placed someone in your life who needs the comfort of your shade? Who is that person? Would you whisper a prayer on his or her behalf? Right now! And what shade tree can you plant in their life at this time?

_____

_____

_____

_____

_____

_____

A turtle on a fence post did not get there by himself. Someone helped him. We did not arrive where we are in life by ourselves either. We all need someone and someone needs us. YES, someone needs you! That truth is revealed in fifty-nine "one another" New Testament phrases. Consider apply-ing a few of these texts. What ACTIONS could you take to fashion the boughs of your life to provide shade for someone else?

John 13:34 – "Love one another."

_____

_____

Romans 12:10 – "Be devoted to one another in brotherly love."

_____

_____

Galatians 5:13 and 6:2 – "Serve one another" and "bear one another's burdens'."

_____

_____

Colossians 3:16 – "With all wisdom teaching and admonishing one another with psalms and hymns and spiritual songs, singing with thankfulness in your hearts to God."

_____

_____

Ephesians 4:2 – "With patience, showing forbearance to one another in love."

_____

_____

Ephesians 4:32 – "Be kind to one another, tender-hearted, forgiving each other."

_____

_____

I Thessalonians 5:11 – "Therefore encourage one another and build up one another."

_____

_____

Hebrews 10:24 – "And let us consider how to stimulate one another to love and good deeds."

_____

_____

Like the redwoods of Muir Woods need each other, believers need one another too! Are you stronger in some areas of life than others? That's why there are times when I need the Christ in you and you need the Christ in me. Maybe you need a dose of Christlike love or patience or forgiveness.

Maybe you need to be an encourager to someone else. What INSIGHTS is God giving you right now?

_____

_____

_____

_____

Alfred Joyce Kilmer was right when he penned, "Poems are made by fools like me, but only GOD CAN MAKE A TREE." Ask the Lord to make you a shade tree today!

SHADE TREE SESSION TWO

PLANTING SHADE TREES
"Sensitivity"

Jeremiah had a spiritual sensitivity to the Spirit of God, to the quiet whispers that we only hear somewhere deep inside (pp. 110–14). Like Elijah hearing that "still small voice" in 1 Kings 19:12, Jeremiah heard the Lord, and it is His voice that we need to hear in the midst of the "voices" that desire our attention.

Three voices beckon for every believer's attention and devotion. First is a DEPRAVED VOICE. That's the voice of our sinful past. The Bible calls it "the flesh" and "self." As believers, we must recognize when "self" begs for attention. According to Galatians 5:17, the flesh constantly "sets its desires" against any element of spiritual transformation. There is also the DEMONIC VOICE. Yes, the Devil is alive, and his motives are revealed in his various names. For example, his name is "tempter" (I Thessalonians 3:5) and the "accuser of the brethren" (Revelation 12:10), and he even transforms himself into an "angel of light" (2 Corinthians 11:14), which points to his deceptive capacity. "Devil" means "false accuser" or "slanderer." Listening to his voice is as foolish as asking Bernie Madoff or another gone-bad Wall Street investor for investment advice! Finally, there is THE DIVINE VOICE.

This is the voice of the Lord. He speaks when we are quiet enough to listen and still enough to hear.

Recall some of those pivotal times in your life that you "heard" the Lord speak to you.

_____

_____

_____

_____

_____

_____

_____

Consider some classic biblical examples of people who were sensitive to the voice of the Lord. Becoming spiritually receptive was a pathway to become shade trees for their generation. Even today we rest under their expanding shade!

Moses was sensitive to the voice of the Lord. What he did next was critical to his future as well as that of an entire nation. Remember Moses and the "burning bush" experience? According to Exodus 3:4, how did Moses reveal he was sensitive to Jehovah's voice?

_____

_____

_____

Samuel was sensitive to the Lord's voice too. His first lesson in the school of spiritual sensitivity is recorded in 1 Samuel 3:1–10. What was Samuel's response to God's call?

_____

_____

_____

After his encounter with the Lord, the prophet Isaiah became sensitive to God's voice too. Find Isaiah 6:1–8. How did his divine encounter affect his sensitivity? What was Isaiah willing to do once he acknowledged the Lord's voice? And, are you "willing" to respond in a like manner, such as Isaiah?

_____

_____

_____

Paul was sensitive to the Spirit too! Acts 16:6–10 records one scene during his second missionary journey where he heard a word from the Lord, "Come over to Macedonia and help us." How did Paul's sensitivity affect others? And how does your "hearing" help others?

_____

_____

_____

Planting shade trees demands we listen to the voice of the Lord only. He spoke then. He speaks today! He is self-revelatory; in other words, He "reveals Himself" for it's His nature. He has given us His Word (the Bible), and He has given us Prayer. He is speaking, and He has something for you to do that no one else can do like you. Find time to talk with Him. Mark 1:35 records that Jesus understood the imperative of having time with God. If the Son of God needed sensitivity, what does that say about you and me?

_____

_____

_____

Dr. Charles Stanley once said, "Your intimacy with God determines your impact on His World." May we hear Him and then plant the shade trees He wants to plant in His behalf!

SHADE TREE SESSION THREE

PLANTING SHADE TREES
"Surrender"

Jeremiah demonstrated surrender for all of us (pp. 115–19). Surrender makes us vulnerable; nevertheless, Jeremiah had a strong belief in surrender with no reserve, no retreat, and no regrets. Jeremiah from his youth led a "surrendered" life to the Lord and His work. And even when Jeremiah found himself in the palace jail (Jeremiah 32), surrendered to the King, he was more importantly surrendered to the Lord in planting shade trees for his people. He bought the field at Anathoth for homes for God's people when they returned from Babylonian exile.

What comes to your mind when thinking of surrender? A white flag? Hands held high above the head? Defeat? In most everything in life, we are taught that surrender is a bad thing. Surrender is for losers. However, that view counters a biblical understanding of life. Jesus described surrender in terms any one of Christ followers may understand. Find Luke 9:23–24. In your own words, write what "surrender" means as a disciple. Surrender is

_____

_____

_____

Jesus teaches that surrender is key to faithfully following Him. It's a paradox of sorts, an oxymoron similar to jumbo shrimp, an accurate stereotype, a new classic, airline food, calm winds, or climb down. Likewise, Jesus is teaching that following Him means we surrender. When we surrender, we WIN, but when we do not surrender, we LOSE. "Whoever loses his life for My sake is the one who will save it."

Can you recall some times when you surrendered and won?

_____

_____

_____

Like lifting a diamond into light reveals brilliant facets of the gem, other biblical writers provide glimpses of the beauty of surrender. There are Paul's words in 1 Corinthians 15:31 and Galatians 6:14. How did he view surrender as a follower of Christ?

_____

_____

As a believer, how do you surrender as a follower of Jesus?

_____

_____

_____

Peter echoes the same view of surrender in 1 Peter 2:21–25. What are some components of surrender from this Christ-follower?

_____

_____

_____

Surrender makes us vulnerable. Surrender runs a risk. Consider Philippians 3:10–21 and how Paul viewed his life as a citizen of heaven yet was willing to flesh it out on this earth. He was so passionate about the things of the Lord he once said that he was willing to be "separated from Christ" so that his kinsmen could be saved! What key words do you notice in Philippians 3:10–21 that reveal Paul's life of surrender?

_____

_____

_____

Are you vulnerable or guarded? Are you willing to risk something, anything for the cause of Christ? Here are a few steps to experiencing the victory of surrender.

1st. LEARN TO HOLD THINGS LOOSELY. When we hold things loosely, it doesn't hurt so much when God, in

His goodness and according to His divine plan, takes those things from us. What do you need to give up today?

_____

_____

_____

2nd. LIVE IN SUCH A WAY THAT ETERNAL THINGS BECOME REAL. Surrender allows us to see our world, ourselves, and our circumstances from an eternal viewpoint. As Christ-followers, the more we surrender the more eternal things become real and earthly things, temporal things, become "unreal." Can you name any eternal things that are becoming more important than your everyday life?

_____

_____

_____

Today, loosen the grip on stuff, on your schedule, on your expectations of others, and even on yourself. Give it all to Jesus! If you lose it, you will find it. While you are at it, ask the Lord to allow you a glimpse of what's really important in life. See it with an eternal view in mind. Surrender is not for losers; it's for those who are more than conquerors in Christ! Give it up . . . all of it!

SHADE TREE SESSION FOUR

PLANTING SHADE TREES
"Silver"

Jeremiah recognized that it took silver to buy the future (pp. 120–23). He took his own stuff, bought a piece of land, and set it aside as a symbol of hope for children who would come back to that land 70 years later. And to top it off, he did this while in jail!

An ancient proverb reminds us, "You cannot take any material goods with you when you die. You should use your money to enjoy yourself when you're alive. Shrouds have no pockets." Irishman Chuck Feeney understands that. This New Jersey native is 80-plus and walks on bad knees. His goal is to die broke. During the past 30 years he has "crisscrossed the globe conducting a clandestine operation to give away his $7.5 billion fortune." The up-and-coming billionaire Bill Gates once told Forbes magazine that "Chuck Feeney is a remarkable role model and the ultimate example of giving while living."

Feeney "gets it." But the fact is, no one has to be a billion-aire in order to be a shade tree in someone else's life. Consider the example of giving by a small band of believers who didn't have two pennies to rub together. Their story is found in 2 Corinthians 8:1–5. Paul is writing to wealthy Corinthians urging them to join in the task of supporting persecuted believers living in Jerusalem. He uses the poor members of Macedonia to illustrate what giving looks like. Find the text and write a couple of insights you discover about giving from this text.

_____

_____

Take special notice that these saints were "begging us with much urging for the favor of participation." In other words, they told Paul, "Include us in this offering!" Remember the scene when Shrek was selecting a traveling companion? It was Donkey who was jumping in the background saying, "Pick me, pick me, pick me!" These broke saints were "begging" and "urging" Paul to pick them too. If this were to occur today, Paul's emails would number into the hundreds. His Facebook account would explode with requests. His cell phone would have dozens of new messages. All of them would sound a similar refrain: "Paul, take an offering for someone else and let me give too!"

Such a spirit of giving would make Chuck Feeney blush. Giving has nothing to do with how much is in a bank account or pocket. It's about attitude. Vision. Greed touches the wealthy man as well as the guy who is "so broke he cannot even pay attention."

Where does a Christ-follower start with giving?

1. LIKE THE MACEDONIANS, GIVE YOURSELF TO THE LORD FIRST. In other words, never allow money, cash, stocks, and retirement accounts be a proxy for following Jesus. Give yourself to the Lord, and you are on the pathway of planting shade trees in the lives of others. Any Insights?

_____

_____

2. LIKE THE MACEDONIANS, SEE GIVING THROUGH EYES OF GRACE, NOT GREED. Why be generous? Why be gracious in giving?

_____

_____

Look no further than the gift God gave to us at Calvary!

3. LIKE THE MACEDONIANS, GIVE WHAT YOU HAVE, NOT WHAT YOU WILL HAVE. The trap in giving looks something like this: "Well, when I get a raise, I will give." "When the stock market is better, I will plant some shade trees." Stop making excuses, and start planting with what you have today.

Remember, you can't take it with you. Grave clothes have no pockets. Be a giver today on this side of the grave. Yes, shade trees cost money! But in the Kingdom Enterprise with God's Economy . . . Who knows, you may live long enough to rest under a shade tree you planted for someone else!

SHADE TREE SESSION FIVE

PLANTING SHADE TREES
"Sight"

*"The only thing worse than being blind
is having sight but no vision."*
Helen Keller

Jeremiah could "see it." Houses, fields, vineyards, . . . and shade trees, if you will. He could see God's people returning from Babylon to their beloved promised land. He therefore invested his SILVER because of his SIGHT.

"Are you blind?" was a comment a disgruntled fan shouted to the umpire. Good question! ARE YOU BLIND? Physical blindness hinders some people, while it creates passion in others. For example, pop artist Stevie Wonder once said, "Just because a man lacks the use of his eyes doesn't mean he lacks vision."

Can you hear the mellow sounds of Ray Charles? He once said, "I don't know what would have happened to me if I hadn't been able to hear."

What do Helen Keller, Ray Charles, and Stevie Wonder have in common? They have vision! Describing the power of vision, George Bernard Shaw once said, "You see things and you say, 'Why?' But I dream of things that never were and I say, 'Why Not?'"

In his book, *Make Your Dreams Come True*, Charles Swindoll describes vision as "essential for survival. It is spawned by faith, sustained by hope, sparked by imagination and strengthened by enthusiasm. It is greater than sight, deeper than a dream, broader than an idea. Vision encompasses vast vistas outside the realm of the predictable, the safe, the unexpected. No wonder we perish without it."

Find Proverbs 29:18. Solomon knew that vision gives us the ability to know how to live. What did Solomon tell us about the power of vision?

_____

_____

_____

Are you blind? Planting a shade tree demands vision. An oak tree comes from a small acorn that is buried in the ground. What do you see in those around you? What do you see in your wife? Your children? Your coworkers? What do you see when you look in the mirror? Do you see opportunity or obstacles? Do you see blessing or cursing? Do you believe or doubt? Confess vision. Today, instead of saying, "I'll believe it when I see it," confess, "I'll see it when I believe it."

SHADE TREE SESSION SIX

PLANTING SHADE TREES
"Signature"

Jeremiah knew that for his "shade tree" (the land of Ana-thoth) to become a reality it would require his signature on the bill of sale. So, in the presence of God's people, the authorities of the day who were the official notaries of his time (Jeremiah 32:12), Jeremiah did not express a vague wish, a whimsical hope, or a cheap desire. He put his name, his life, his character on the line. With his name, he pledged to buy the property and left a public record of what he had done. And we grow under his influence today because he "signed on" to the kingdom work of God (pp. 131–44).

Take a look at it this way. When you sit down to breakfast and you order ham and eggs, remember this: one is a contribution (the eggs), and the other is a total commitment (the ham). A hen gives while a pig is all in! That's the difference in some believers too! Too many of us want to add to something instead of giving it all.

Are you all in? Jim Elliot was one of five missionaries killed while participating in Operation Auca as they were attempting to evangelize the Huaorani people of Ecuador. Elliot once said, "Wherever you are, be all there. Live to the hilt every situation you believe to be the will of God."

When thinking about commitment, remember anything about 212? That number is the difference between boiling water and steam. Water under heat simply boils at temperatures under 212 degrees, but steam is created at 212 degrees Fahrenheit. Steam has more energy. That's why a steam burn is worse than water burns. Steam moves while water remains in a pot. One is released; the other sits!

Are you operating your faith at 210 or 211 degrees? Spiritually speaking, anything less than 212 degrees faith is LUKEWARM. Jesus highlighted lukewarmness in Revelation 3:15–16. What is lukewarmness to you?

_____

_____

_____

Pray that "lukewarm" never describes your walk with the Lord! Jim Elliot would tell us to "live to the hilt." Give it all. Be all in, like the framers of the Constitution, like the brave defenders inside the walls of the Alamo, and like Jesus whose passion and purpose was "to seek and save that which was lost." It's time to sign on the line. It's time for you to be "all in."

One thing about a signature . . . it's yours! And you sign your name on many things: a driver's license, paperwork for a new car and a new home, and all kinds of business documents. But your signature on the sacred activity of Planting Shade Trees (some that you will never sit under) will be celebrated not only on this earth but also praised over in eternity. So, SIGN UP . . . SIGN ON . . . until we SIGN OFF!

Evangelist D. L. Moody once said, "The world has yet to see what God can do with a man fully consecrated to him." Ask the Lord to make you that kind of Shade Tree Christ Follower. A 212 follower. A guy who lives to the hilt. Along the way, you will plant a forest of shade trees!

A BRIEF WORD ABOUT
SWANBERG CHRISTIAN MINISTRIES

I know that you are going to enjoy *Planting Shade Trees* in a variety of family and faith avenues. If the Lord ever directs you to help us at SCM in our MINISTRY OF ENCOURAGEMENT, just know that we appreciate your consideration. Swanberg Christian Ministries is a non-profit ministry, and we seek to encourage the saints now that His day is drawing near. (Heb. 10:25). We also have strong mission ties and partnerships with specific missionary evangelists in Southeast Asia and Philippines, as well as general missions associated with the International Mission Board. We are also blessed to encourage our UNITED STATES MILITARY. The Lord has directed our paths to Iraq, Germany, South Korea, and Middle East. Doors have continued to open up at military bases stateside—we enjoy giving them support and encouragement.

Swanberg Christian Ministries
www.dennisswanberg.com
Swanbergministries@gmail.com
318-325-9044 office

ABOUT THE AUTHOR

Dennis Swanberg served the local church in pastoral ministry for 23 years. Then, in 1995, Dennis took a leap of faith when he stepped down as church pastor and stepped up to the microphone. Soon, Swan became "America's Minister of Encouragement," a job he takes seriously as he continues to speak to about 150 churches and organizations every year. He has hosted two successful TV series, authored eight books, and created over a dozen DVDs.

Dennis is a graduate of Baylor University where he majored in both Greek and religion (1976). He earned both a Master of Divinity (1980) and a Doctor of Ministry (1986) at Southwestern Seminary, Ft. Worth, Texas.

Dennis is married to Lauree Wilkes of Ft. Worth. He has two grown sons: Chad and Dusty. The Swans make their home in Monroe, Louisiana.

If you would like to book Dr. Swanberg to speak for your church, organization, or corporate group, please feel free to contact him by phone at 318-325-9044 or e-mail him at Swanbergministries@gmail.com. You can also begin the process of booking the Swan on his web site, www.dennisswanberg.com. You can also find Dr. Swanberg's other BOOKS AND PRODUCTS at his ministry website.